Hugh Casson's London

For M and our daughters Carola, Nicola and Dinah

HUGH CASSON'S
LONDON

J. M. Dent & Sons Ltd
London   Melbourne

The author and publishers wish to thank the following for permission to reproduce certain paintings in this book: Joanna Brendon and The Friends of St John's Smith Square for the illustration of 'St John's Smith Square'; Lord Birkett and the GLC for 'Holland House Park'; IBM for 'Burlington House'; and James Bishop and *The Illustrated London News* for 'Wormwood Scrubs', 'The Debenham House', 'Highgate Cemetery', 'Stanley Gardens', 'The Albert Memorial' and 'Carlton House Terrace'. Jacket photograph of Sir Hugh Casson by Paul Caffell.

This book originated as a publishing project of the K. S. Giniger Company, Inc., New York City.

First published 1983
Reprinted 1983
Reprinted 1985
© Hugh Casson 1983

This book is set in 11/13 Monophoto Bembo by
Jolly & Barber Ltd, Rugby
Printed in Italy by
Imago Publishing Ltd, Thame, for
J.M. Dent & Sons Ltd
Aldine House, 33 Welbeck Street, London W1M 8LX

British Library Cataloguing in Publication Data

Casson, *Sir* Hugh
    Hugh Casson's London.
    1. London (England)—Description—1951-   —Views.
    I. Title
    942.1085′8′0222   DA684.2

ISBN 0-460-04591-1

Contents

Introduction 6

Part One

Round Pond 10
No. 4 Crossfield Road 12
Selfridges 14
Cheyne Walk 17
Queen Anne's Gate 20
Maida Hill West 22
Gower Street 24
Bedford Square 26
Hammersmith Bridge 28
Lloyd Square, Clerkenwell 30
Greenwich 32
Charlotte Street 34
The Debenham House–
    8 Addison Road 36
The Albert Memorial 38
Old Church Street, Chelsea 40
Mary Ward Settlement 42
Hampton Court 44
St Margaret's Westminster 46

Part Two

The Boat House, Syon 48
Syon House 50
South Bank 52
The Royal Albert Hall 54
Thurloe Place, South Kensington 56
Holland House Park 58
Tower Bridge 60
Buckingham Palace 62
St John's, Smith Square 64
Chiswick Mall 66
St Mary's Battersea 68
Leighton House 69
Portobello Road 72
Euston Road Fire Station 74
Windsor Castle 76
The Palace Theatre 78
The Natural History Museum 80
Marylebone Station 82
The National Portrait Gallery 84
Burlington House 86
The Royal College of Music 88
Blewcoat School 90
Wormwood Scrubs 92
The Sir John Soane Museum 94
Dulwich Art Gallery 96
Elephant House, London Zoo 98
Turner's House, Twickenham 100
The Royal Mint 102
Carlton House Terrace 104
Olympia 106
18 Stafford Terrace 108
Platt's Lane, Hampstead 110
Palace of Westminster 112
Highgate Cemetery 114
Stanley Gardens 116
County Hall 118
Holly Village 120
The Royal Opera House,
    Covent Garden 122
The National Theatre 124
Harrow 126

Introduction

I was born in London and have lived in London virtually all my working life. London is the home of our children and grandchildren. This may sound like total immersion, but it's more like hitching a ride on the Leviathan. I live, it seems, like a comfortably housed stowaway on a great liner, seldom leaving my familiar deck-cabin or companion-way, while the great ship itself, upperworks agleam, flags flying and portholes blazing, thunders and shudders impassively on its way through the seasons and the years.

As a child I knew London only through the occasional visit . . . the Zoo, Gamages, 'Where the Rainbow Ends' . . . either with parents when, too rarely, on leave from India, or with relatives, or, if they ran short, in the care of 'Universal Aunts' – a sedate middle-class escort agency which flourished between the wars. On our London visits, my sister and I always stayed with our Great-Aunt Torie in Montagu Street – a sort of clearing house and information centre for the huge numbers of aunts and uncles and cousins passing regularly through London 'en route' to or from service in the Empire. Great-Aunt Torie was unmarried and comfortably off. She was about seventy I suppose but seemed to me incredibly old. (She boasted once she had been taken in to dinner by Disraeli who wore rings over his gloves.) She was tended by three maids – Ada, Bird and Mary – all as old as she – who for us acted as the patient, warm-hearted bollards round which we threw our ropes of childish confidence. Often indeed we found it hard to leave the friendly basement kitchen in which Ada and Bird, stiffly corsetted and aproned, tacked creaking and rustling round the table like great yachts, while Mary, who was tiny, fluttered like a pinnace between them.

Outside, humming to itself like some great engine, was London . . . which to me meant Oxford Street and even more particularly Selfridges. Selfridges was my passion. In those days – the early 'twenties – the lift girls were clothed in mauve riding habits – breeches, gaiters and white gold-pinned cravats. Strange mauve hats, pleated and peaked, were perched upon their curls. Impassive, imperious, glassy-eyed, miraculous, they ruled their tiny palaces (the golden lift gates are now in the London Museum) like goddesses in a Handel opera. No place on earth – not even the Hornby section of Gamages – was so glorious as Selfridges . . . and if you wanted adventure-plus, there were in Oxford Street 'pirate buses' – private enterprise vehicles that at your signal, even a child's, would swoop to the kerb and pick you up under the steaming radiator nose of the official LGOC line.

It was at Montagu Street that my sister and I were initiated into the ritualistic life patterns of middle-class Londoners . . . meals, in one room or another, striking as punctually as the gongs that announced their arrival . . . afternoon calls . . . coal scuttles brought up, trays taken down . . . curtains drawn back or closed – everything as regular as a minuet. We quickly found our own unchanging rhythm . . . breakfast in the kitchen . . . '*Have you been yet?*' . . . playing with the service lift . . . Selfridges . . . lunch . . . rest . . . Selfridges or Hyde Park . . . tea . . . reading *The Railway Children* in the bay window . . . biscuits and bed. It was a foretaste of the future. To the eyes of a child, London, for all its size and murmur, seemed a tiny enclosed world, seldom strayed from, dependable in its attractions, strictly defined in its frontiers between poverty and wealth, architecturally logical (bricks for houses, pointed windows for churches, columns for commerce) and thus providing comfortingly recognisable landmarks to guide you home.

In later years – after retiring from India my father had become a lecturer at Southampton University – my visits to London became more schoolboy-solitary. They were easy to arrange. Rival bus companies ran daily trips to London (5/- return fare) and such was the competition they would pick you up and drop you back at home like giant taxis. Those trips, perhaps two each holiday, were escapes from home – the normal need to be occasionally alone – rather than searches for metropolitan adventure. When, after that four-hour drive, we reached London I never visited 'a sight' such as the Tower or Westminster Abbey. I just walked the streets, savouring that wonderful feeling (wonderful of course only if you have security and love behind you) of being alone, unknown and on your own, among a thousand others . . . and elated, too, by the knowledge that London wasn't just another city – a place larger than Southampton – but it was where it all *was* even if you couldn't actually catch sight of it . . . and so the whole place became a sort of World Fair, with strange pavilions and devices at every turn, clamorous, crowded, dizzying the eyes.

Late adolescence brought another change of attitudes towards London. Undergraduate trips in term-time – brief, infrequent, nervous – meant Tutor's permissions and *exeats*. By now, too, the need not to be solitary but to be part of a group encouraged a new self-conscious, self-advertising behaviour – larky clothing and noisy car exhausts. Sporting those badges of timidity – long, striped college scarves – we gathered defiantly outside pubs in our plus-fours. Terrified of tarts, frightened of waiters, uncertain of where everything was, we would, in the end, find sanctuary in a Corner House or a cinema. London this time looked a lot bigger and a lot less easy to deal with.

Not until 1932 did I start to become a Londoner – somebody who lives and works in London. I was still a period piece – conventional in taste, nervous of experiment, 'sheltered', like Roy Fuller, 'from poverty and hurt, from passion, tragedy and dirt'. The idea of spending a vacation as a *plongeur* at the Ritz or as an assistant at Woolworth's was inconceivable. Vacations were spent at home or staying with friends. It was a soft, enjoyable, if rather smuggish existence, but London (and this was its glory) didn't care . . . so nor did we.

A fellow-architectural student, F., and I set up house together – first in Chelsea, then in Maida Vale, finally in Paddington. We were completing our studies in Bloomsbury . . . far away to the east it seemed and the London in-between remained, since we were curiously incurious, largely unvisited. It did not take us long to discover that, although to the historian – and also to the visitor – London still seems a collection of villages separately identifiable, to the workers it is more like a close-knit pattern of connections as familiar, well-trodden and ritualistic even as the forest paths and clearings of a savage tribe. Home, work, lunch place, pub, local supermarket and restaurant are all reference points to be recognised every day. The smallest disturbance, a road diversion, a shop closing, the sacking of a waitress, is as unwelcome as a blow. A bus strike is treated not as a chance to stay at home but as a challenge to get to work at the usual time and keep the thread unbroken.

You could despise all this punctual, unwavering, accepted regularity as being the prison of 'the rat race' (and indeed it can be stifling to the young) or taking the other view, you could enjoy it as 'the miracle of normality' . . . that flywheel of the usual that keeps our lives balanced and our thoughts at ease. There are as many who hug their handcuffs to their hearts as those who dream of future release, and Simone Weil was not the first to discover (what in fact many men and surely every woman knows) that it is from our physical roots that we draw our social and intellectual strength, and when such roots are destroyed by apathy or violence or money mania, the results can be catastrophic. Every man's London therefore can only be a small one, torn and patched by events and changes in personal life but linked by familiar threads and signal systems and marker buoys, as small as a creaking gate or as imposing as a viaduct. As an architect, I am ashamed to admit that my own 'familiar' London still scarcely exceeds five miles in circumference . . . from Hampstead to the river and from Covent Garden to Chiswick. Even within that area there are acres and acres of streets and buildings that I have never, in fifty years of London-living, set eyes on – nor probably ever will. To describe it as 'My London' sounds pretentious as well as untruthful . . . yet, although it is shared by thousands, it is nobody else's . . . quite.

If 'My' London, as seen in the following pages, seems to be not only tiny in area, socially uniform – no Bethnal Green or Wandsworth – haphazard and arbitrary in its choice of subject – why the Palace Theatre rather than the National? – so anecdotal rather than scholarly in its information – what is the relevance of my great-aunt's cook or the dancing skill of Lord Leighton PRA? – I can only reply that this is a personal picture book of buildings that I have grown to like or admire, that have had some connection, however fragile, with some event, experience or period in my life, and that are enjoyable to draw (modern architecture can be exciting to look at but is seldom fun to draw). I find concentrated information – names and dates pattering down like rain on a car roof – as dull as a diet of gravel, so that the only point of compiling a book like this is to enjoy doing it.

In choosing what to draw I have been aware that, like everybody else, I am lashed – who isn't? – to the wheel of taste, liking things today that I disliked yesterday and may dislike again tomorrow. In my younger days the Hoover Factory was not a monument but a tasteless joke, and who (as yet) stands in admiration before that award-winning flat-block of the 'fifties? We all look through spectacles, one lens of which seems beyond our control. The buildings I have illustrated come in all shapes, sizes and styles, but most of them were built between 1830 and 1930 –

architecturally a period of great creative confidence when you can sense somebody is in charge and when it was not thought absurdly extravagant to enrich a façade with bay windows and sculptures or enliven a roof silhouette with spires and cupolas, even just for the fun of it.

As to the anecdotal captions, it can only be said again this is not a history of, nor guide to, London – only some personal portraits of some of its buildings and how they came into being. A date and an architect's name may provide the core of the fruit but, to get the flavour, the knowledge that the client was a crook or the architect a non-conformist may not be irrelevant. Every building after all is a battlefield, a three-dimensional map of compromise, victory or defeat, stained with the blood of the participants, and the more you know about the background of the fighters, the better you understand and enjoy the building.

Even in this image-drunk age, looking at buildings, or as Ruskin so perceptively advised, 'watching' them, is a pastime reserved by most people for weekends and holidays, and choices are safely confined to the old Medieval Abbey, the National Trust House, the picture postcard village. Few people can describe the physical face of the office block in which they work or remember what the local town hall is made of. For most eyes, the blinkers were fastened on at school. To hint at an interest in architecture was to invite the well-meant instruction from the schoolmaster to go and look at a font rather than say the new bus-station. The first is 'Architecture', the second a three-dimensional facility to be used rather than looked at. Once on the nose, the blinkers remain until temporarily readjusted, perhaps by some local conservation issue when a judgment and a vote is demanded. Even women – whose eye for what every passer-by is wearing is always pin-sharp – usually fail the architectural observer test.

Meanwhile the professionals soldier on getting things built and battling with bureaucracy, learning new technical tricks, exchanging in-talk and trying on one stylistic hat after another . . . Bauhaus in the 'thirties . . . the tiptoe 'fifties and the blockhouse 'sixties . . . the Peasant versus High-Tech of the 'seventies . . . the neo-Classicism of the 'eighties, while their professional press, like Madame Tussaud, is kept busy melting down yesterday's heroes to remodel today's. No wonder the non-professional prefers to keep his blinkers on and leave the game of building to the experts – letting yet one more human activity, like teaching the young and the care of the old, go over to those who are paid to get it done. No wonder maybe . . . but no fun either. For architecture, whether you regard it as no more than large-scale problem-solving or as a visible system of three-dimensional ideas, is there – hard as it may seem to believe this sometimes – to be enjoyed and to be looked at.

Here anyway are sixty buildings of my choice . . . some famous, some I hope unknown, and some so familiar that they are no longer observed. Familiarity does not breed contempt so much as blindness – who if challenged can remember quickly and off-hand a list of the pictures in his own entrance hall? They are inevitably an odd lot but I have enjoyed drawing them, and hope that the results will be enjoyed enough by others to encourage them if not to go and see the buildings for themselves, to look at all buildings with a sharper and more appreciative eye.

Round Pond. Kensington Gardens.

PART ONE

No 4 Crossfield Road

According to H.G. Wells, the Victorian suburb was an ingenious weapon designed for the subjection of women. (Certainly it was founded on belief in their inferiority.) Crossfield Road is a typical example. It lies in a pleasantly indecisive no-man's-land between Regent's Park and South Hampstead. It was developed at a leisurely pace largely by two speculative builders, Cuming and Willett, between 1820 and 1900 and (to the delight of the landlords – Eton College) proved to be a steady success. It is a middling sort of place built for middling people – sober, respectable, conventional and thrifty. The absence of mews and the scarcity of shops and pubs show that the working classes were to be kept at arms' length and the architectural formula of stucco and brick – described by later historians as mediocre, commonplace and catchpenny – solid-looking without and precarious within, exactly fitted the required image of privacy made more secure by social cohesion.

By the end of the century, however, this cosy crust had begun to crumble. Every family house had become a lodging house, a private hotel, a nest of flatlets. (They could be nothing else because there was nothing else to be.) Kitchenettes were being wedged on half-landings. Geyser flues and waste pipes sprouted through upper windows. Bells subscribed with faded name-labels erupted by the front doors. No 4, where I was born in 1910, had become – behind its striped grey façade, perky Gothic detail and formidable porch and half-careened gate piers – a modest nursing home. I left it one week old in the arms of a kindly aunt and did not see the house again until I did the drawing opposite.

14

Selfridges

Selfridges was built in stages.—
+ several architects were employed—
All followed the original classical
concept established by Frank
Atkinson. + given his own
personal stamp in the detailing.

Two great department stores rule over London – Selfridges in Oxford Street and Harrods in Knightsbridge – one Roman in its classical magnificence, the other Byzantine in its richness and elaborate silhouette. Much as I still enjoy their architecture, I seldom enter either, but there was a time when such places were as enthralling as any museum or exhibition. Shops are show business and the best ones are the children of their impresarios.

Gordon Selfridge was one of the greatest of these – a successful and ambitious junior partner in the great Chicago store of Marshall Field but with his eye on London. In 1906 he arrived here to set up shop. In 1908 he bought a site in Oxford Street - not then a fashionable shopping street – and a year later he opened up . . . 130 departments, carpeted throughout, brilliantly lighted and staffed by the highest-paid shop assistants in London. He spent nearly a million pounds on advertising, and introduced a bargain basement, a roof garden, and annual sales. He encouraged people to browse as well as to buy and by 1914 it was an established success. By 1920 Selfridges was twice its original size (the new architects Graham Anderson Robert & White stuck to the great classical design set up by its original designer Frank Atkinson, although the authorities refused to allow the hoped-for central tower or dome). In 1936 the six-ton clock of Time (designed by Gilbert Bayes) was hoisted into its central position and in 1937 Selfridge spent nearly £50,000 on the store's Coronation decorations.

He was always a big spender on promotional projects, and the money began to dribble out as fast as it dribbled in. After the Second World War he was voted off the board and the store – though still autonomous – has passed through a sequence of holding groups.

Selfridge died in 1947, leaving an enterprise which is, architecturally at least, still the flagship of Oxford Street, its jumbo-sized columns and cornices striking down the side-streets like temple gongs. Selfridge and his architect knew that architecture is more than problem-solving – more even than providing a proper setting for some activity. It must also serve as a symbol. Here it had to stand for quality, confidence, reliability and permanence but not, curiously enough considering the client, for quick-moving and modish enterprise. (Selfridge was one of the first retailers to sell clothes as fashion and not for everlasting wear.) But it's paid off. The gimcrack architectural argot that is spoken the length of Oxford Street expresses only too clearly the short-lived, hard-edged, thin-skinned quality of Ad-land. (Did Selfridge, I wonder, invent perhaps the gift department, the place to get what nobody wants either to buy or to receive?) It's easy of course to be a smarty-pants about Oxford Street . . . its aimlessly drifting, paperbag-clutching crowds, its flash shop fronts, its fume-clotted air, its almost totally despairing architecture – roof it over and it would become one huge department store – but it lives up to its role as a spectacle as well as a market place and recognises, I suspect, that Selfridges is still the star of the show.

Cheyne Walk

For me no day is happily complete without sight of a stretch of water – even if it be no larger than the Serpentine – and masts at the end of a street are the essential ingredient of a city worth living in ('Sky and water', said Turner, 'are they not glorious?'). So when leaving university in 1931 I was determined to live as near water as I could find and could afford. A fellow-student and I found rooms at the shabbiest end of Cheyne Walk over looking the boatyards, and lived there happily until driven inland by a rival tide . . . of Embankment traffic.

But although we reluctantly deserted the place for a time – an emotional farewell to our red-haired landlady called (unbelievably) Mrs Fallus – this stretch of waterfront remained woven into my life. Two of my great Victorian heroes, Brunel and Turner, lived here (Turner secretly under the pseudonym of 'Puggy' Booth), plus other favourite painters, John Martin, Whistler and Walter Greaves. Lindsey House (No 96) once the headquarters of the Moravian sect, was a hospitable home for me and many friends during the V bombs. Opposite stood Battersea Bridge River Fire Station (now vanished) where in 1938 I was trained as a river fireman and where, for a few months in 1940, I was stationed, learning to work a switchboard and to man a fire pump-barge. Just downriver is Battersea Park, the site of the Festival Fun Fair in 1951 – and the nightmare, caused by weather, of its delayed construction. Opposite again is St Mary's Battersea, one of my favourite London churches, commanding an upriver reach, and further on is the beautifully restored Old Battersea House, crammed to the brim by its owner Christopher Forbes with fine Pre-Raphaelite paintings and early twentieth-century ship models.

No wonder Chelsea waterfront always attracted writers and artists – George Eliot and Thomas Carlyle, Rossetti, Oscar Wilde, Leigh Hunt, John Sargent. A few studios remain – but not many containing practising artists. The streets and squares that run inland are full of 'people who have arrived before they got there'. King's Road, feverishly hot-eyed in pursuit of its reputation, the glaring red-faced gables of Pont Street . . . all begin to lose their allure. But not this corner. The house boats creak and grumble on the tide, the flower boxes shift uneasily on the cabin roofs, the flags and washing flick angrily at the sea-gulls, the light reflected from the water dances gently on the underside of awnings. There is a smell of mud and paint.

— Low Tide
The Yacht Yard
Cheyne Walk · Chelsea

Queen Anne's Gate

Every Wednesday morning, for something like twenty years – interrupted only by the war – I spent in No 9 Queen Anne's Gate, the office of the Architectural Press, first as an anonymous contributor to, and later editor of, a weekly column, and then joining Sir James Richards and Sir Nikolaus Pevsner on the editorial Board of England's premier monthly, the *Architectural Review*. Pevsner, a brisk, spectacled dynamo who knew the date and derivation of everything, kept us clear on the scholarly front. Richards, trained as an architect, was the experienced executive editor. Rather like my predecessor, Sir Osbert Lancaster, I was a fringe figure. All three of us were subject to the inventive but unpredictably explosive whims of the chairman, H. de C. Hastings, a crusty, brilliant eccentric – as hot-tempered, mercurial, lovable and infuriating as an editor in a movie. He had a sharp eye for talent – he gave John Betjeman his first job as a journalist and personally illustrated his first book of poems – cared passionately for architecture, though not at all for architects, and divided his time between his Sussex farm (where the animals, from cows to goats, were selected to match the scale of the fields in which they grazed) and his office at No 9 which he transformed behind its sedate, sash-windowed façade into a mirrored, dark-stained, jackdaw's nest ruled over by a stuffed lion. Here, deer-stalkered and hounds-toothed, he sat drinking hock and selzer, writing pamphlets and leaders, commissioning artists to illustrate his brainwaves, recalling for rewriting whole issues already sent to press. He would disappear for months at a time then reappear with thousands of words and almost as many photographs.

No sign of this fantasy figure nor of his self-made setting disturb the serenity of Queen Anne's Gate – one of the best preserved bits of early eighteenth-century domestic architecture in London (1705) – garden-wall-coloured bricks, black railings, white window bars and elaborately carved canopies over the panelled entrance doors, huddled like the houses in a cathedral close in the shadow of modern office blocks. Large-scale speculative building after the Great Fire encouraged uniformity, and London houses from 1666–1730 all looked much the same. The windows are indeed all the same size – no grand first floor – and ornament is kept to keystones, door hoods and cornices. A statue of Queen Anne – said to have been intended for the church of St Mary-le-Strand – commands the twist in the street, and the clock-tower of Big Ben strikes down the eastern approach alley.

Maida Hill West

Driven inland by the thunder of the Embankment's traffic F. and I sought water again – this time in Maida Vale. In those days the canal was a secret and melancholy place concealed beneath a dark tunnel of trees, the water's surface – the colour of polished boots – only occasionally disturbed by a working narrow-boat put-putting its way to Birmingham. No weekend boat rallies, no floating art galleries, no Zoo waterbus, no smart little cruisers with the kettle on the boil behind the cretonne curtains. We took rooms in a square, stuccoed villa, lofty sash windows set into a pale, flatly modelled façade. The claws of a tiny yellow Pomeranean dog belonging to the landlady scrabbled and clicked endlessly on the linoed landings, and in winter a mist rose from the water and penetrated the house, leaving a misty bloom on the mahogany stair-rail.

The house was full of lodgers – a painter, two fellow-students, a journalist with a Dutch mistress who once – ah, the sophistication of it! – came into the bathroom to talk to me while I was having a bath. Just beyond us the canal opened out into Paddington basin, lined with deserted wharves and huge stuccoed houses – crumbling cornices, trickling wastepipes, rusty fire-escapes – that seemed about to collapse into their own reflections. Everywhere that smell of water that is occasionally disturbed but never changed. Here, among the slipping slates and patched plaster, the title 'Little Venice' seemed more appropriate than further east where the villas, ranked primly behind their garden walls, gazed at each other with an English lack of warmth. At one end of our little stretch lay a bridge and the lock-keeper's cottage awash with delphiniums, at the other end the long dripping tunnel to King's Cross. This had been built in 1802 when it was decided – to the rage of the Paddington Wharfingers – to extend the canal right down to the London Docks, a ten-year-old idea that had to await the driving support of John Nash to become a reality. Nash, with his engineer-colleague Morgan, took an active hand in the route – taking it round the north boundary of Marylebone Fields (now Regent's Park) and also persuading his royal patron to call it the Regent Canal. By 1820 it was all complete, its only subsequent excitement being the blowing up by anarchists in 1874 of a bridge near the Zoo, an explosion which broke the glass in Alma Tadema's studio across the road.

Gower Street

Gower Street – built like an inverted Venetian canal (the road is at a higher level than the back gardens each side of it) – has always lacked friends. The Victorians thought it hideously dull, reserving praise only for the north end where University College Hospital – a spiky brick-and-faience cruet, the colour of dried blood – stares at University College, where I spent my final two years as a student.

We took little notice of its architecture. Even architectural students are less interested in the scenery at their backs than in the play and the players. For us the point was to be in London, never mind where or what it looked like. For that matter we seldom visited the British Museum or the great monuments of London – Greenwich or the Tower or the Wren Churches or the National Gallery.

The drawing studio was large and crowded. Of the hundred or so students perhaps a dozen were women (including my future wife). The Professor was the celebrated Richardson, a hook-nosed, sallow-wattled, voluble enthusiast for the eighteenth century (he was alleged to wear buckled shoes when at home), who enlivened his lectures not with slides but with his own electrically cursive drawings done at high speed before your very eyes. On the ground floor – some university eye must have drooped or winked – an enterprising administrative officer called Stanley operated for a fee a highly efficient correspondence crash-course for students in a hurry or in difficulties. Life was pleasant enough. Lectures and design exercises occupied our days. We ate at Bertorelli's, went home at weekends, hitching lifts in friends' cars. We had little contact with the Slade School next door (except to goggle at the girls sitting on the sunlit steps), hardly ever entered the centre domed building that tries to command the courtyard of UCL. Only in the last two years – when struggling with the problems of completing the Gower Street frontage – have I returned to take a serious look at the place, and I found it more interesting than I had remembered . . . but not much.

The architect of the centre block, William Wilkins, the busy and successful son of an architect, had been educated at Cambridge. He designed Downing College, perhaps his best work, in 1810 at the age of twenty-six, he was a prim and rather pedantic admirer of Greek revivalism (St George's Hospital and the National Gallery are among his later works), but seemed to lack assurance. Although the central flight of steps is impressive, the columns look crowded and the dome inadequate – instinctively you heighten it when you draw it. Nevertheless that glimpse of green, the parade of dignified windows, the perky little lodges and observatories are very welcome in a street otherwise enlivened only in my memory by the occasional glimpse of the wide-brimmed hats of Lady Ottoline Morrell or Lady Diana Cooper coming out of the local dairy. No wonder all schemes to close off this view have foundered.

Bedford Square

In 1630 the 4th Earl of Bedford created in Covent Garden, London's first formally designed open space. About 150 years later Bedford Square was laid out at the south end of Bloomsbury - dignified, formal, discreet. Arched doorways, elegant sash windows, Coade keystones, handsome railings, large trees. It would be no surprise, even today, to meet here a sedan chair. On the west side are Nos 34–36 built for the Bedford family by Robert Crews and William Scott. Since 1917 these houses have been the home of the Architectural Association, founded in 1842 by a group of young architectural pupils with the simple aim of self-improvement. The subscription was £1 a year. Meetings were held every fortnight. Four years later two ambitious and spirited young students, Robert Kell and Charles Gray (Gray was eighteen, Kell was twenty-three) decided the Association needed waking up. They decided the pupilage system was a fraud, that the RIBA was a gang of tradesmen, that they and their lively young friends would have to start their own school. Seminars and lectures were organised, visits arranged, design projects set.

In 1859 the AA joined forces with another group of architectural dissidents and moved to Conduit Street. By 1866 they were over the hump. All the administration was done by volunteers. Classes were held regularly and so successfully that by 1887 the AA was beginning to outgrow its strength and in 1889 it was reorganised. Problems of curriculum, examinations and premises were debated and after a couple of intermediate moves the AA came to anchor in Bedford Square, where it now resides. A five-year course was started, the evening school closed, the slump survived. The traditional vitality of this self-governing school flared up again in the mid-'thirties, was temporarily doused by the war and has returned to enliven the architectural world through the last thirty or so years. The eighteenth-century houses contain the inner excitement without blinking.

Hammersmith Bridge

For three years I knew the underside of Hammersmith Bridge better than the top. As cox to my college eight in the 'thirties, I was often on the tideway practising for some race or other and Hammersmith – like Harrods Repository – was a marker point for stop watches and purple-faced megaphoning coaches. I've always enjoyed the elaborate gaiety of the design – particularly since it has been so splendidly painted up. It's one of those bridges that leaps rather than stumps across the river. The designer was Sir Joseph Bazalgette and it was built 1884–7 on the piers of the original bridge. The bridge is carried on wrot iron chains suspended from cast-iron and turretted towers. Sir Joseph, who should in justice be as well known as Christopher Wren or John Nash, was one of London's forgotten achievers. He was Chief Engineer of the Metropolitan Board of Works in the 1860s – the great age of underground railways and sewers.

London then was a huge building site. Four great sewers ploughed from east to west. The District and Inner Circle Lines were under construction, so were all the main termini and the railways and bridges that served them. (Of the three million inhabitants, nearly 100,000 were employed on building.) Two enormous and architecturally elaborate pumping stations – both today visitable – were built by Sir Joseph at Crossness (1865) and Abbey Mills (1868), the Victoria & Albert Embankment was completed in 1870, and Chelsea Embankment a few years later (there's a memorial to him at the foot of Northumberland Avenue). He was responsible for Putney and Battersea Bridge, investing everything he touched, however mundane, with an engaging swagger. A great man.

Lloyd Square, Clerkenwell

One of the nicest squares in London . . . early nineteenth-century, privately owned, within sight of the spires of St Pancras. The houses stand linked arm-in-arm, so to speak, guarding their well-kept simplicity from the roar of Rosebery Avenue and King's Cross Road. Lloyd Square is a minor masterpiece of understated elegance and not surprisingly it was one of the building groups I was sent to draw as a student. It has not changed a whisker since, at least from the outside, although here and there behind the hand-painted blinds can be glimpsed the spoor of colour-supplement life.

The Square – part of a 15-acre estate – has been owned by one family, the Lloyd Bakers of Gloucestershire, since 1828 – and still is. Miss Lloyd Baker who watched over the estate from 1916 until her death in 1975 ran it like a feudal village. She had no use for landlords who treated property as an investment and not as a responsibility. She prided herself on knowing every one of her 450 tenants. They were carefully chosen and frequently visited. Properties were regularly inspected, the condition of the gardens and changes in wallpaper noted. Birthdays were remembered, marriages recorded. She seems to have been kind and courteous, perceptive and respected.

Strangely enough for so well-run an estate no evidence seems to exist as to who designed and built these charming little villas. Sir John Summerson believes that probably either Thomas Cubitt, the builder of Belgravia, or his brother William, was responsible – their headquarters were nearby and the dates are right – between 1825 and 1830. Full marks anyway to those who built Lloyd Square and to the family that have looked after it so well and for so long.

Greenwich

Five miles below London Bridge lies Greenwich, the site of the Tudor Palace of Placentia, Henry VIII's first palace till he moved upstream to Hampton Court. Anne Boleyn left here for execution and Queen Elizabeth I was born here. The Stuarts abandoned Placentia but James II returned to build the Queen's House, a formal little summer palace set astride the Woolwich Road and designed in his latest Italian manner by Inigo Jones. It remains the tiny focus of a magnificent architectural set-piece composed by Christopher Wren and to which all the three great Baroque architects – Webb, Vanbrugh and Hawksmoor – contributed. By European standards – Paris, Rome or St Petersburg – it was all modest enough but for England, always ill at ease in the presence of rhetoric, it is stupendous . . . four great quadrangles, four balanced blocks each named for a sovereign, two sentinel domes guarding the Chapel and the Great Hall painted by Thornhill (he got £1 a foot for walls and £3 a foot for ceilings) – the whole with its grassy backdrop and dotty little off-centre observatory (every day at 1pm a red ball is raised and lowered), all best seen, as Canaletto saw it, from the North Bank (reached incidentally by a splendidly sinister underwater tunnel). Linked to the Queen's House by open colonnades are the nineteenth-century buildings of the National Maritime Museum (opened 1934), for my money the most splendid museum in London and of its kind surely the best in the world.

There's plenty else to see in Greenwich: bits – not many – of the old town, the dry-docked *Cutty Sark* and *Gypsy Moth*, the parish church of St Alphege by Hawksmoor, and at the top of Crown's Hill above the river the seventeenth-century Ranger's House. (One of the last Rangers, though she lived nearby in Montague House, was poor Queen Caroline, the plump, spirited and rejected wife of the Prince Regent. Here, it was said, she entertained her lover, an Admiral called Smith, so tiny that it was claimed you could see the top of his head down Queen Caroline's décolletage.) Plenty of good terraces and villas surround the windy heath but there's more fun down the river along the newly opened and highly recommended walk. You need a day for Greenwich. Take a boat from Westminster and a picnic to the top of the hill and watch the Thames wind gracefully upriver to Westminster – and eastward to the sea.

Charlotte Street

To us as students in the 'thirties, Charlotte Street was a substitute Montparnasse, the haunt (or so we believed) of the true Bohemians, the Royal Court of ill-kempt, self-assured, pub-crawling performers, presided over in spirit or in fact by Augustus John (who lived at No 76 – the old house of Constable) and who seemed to us to live a life of enviable disdain for conformity. We worshipped at two temples – the Fitzroy and Bertorelli's. Never at ease in pubs, I was nervous of the Fitzroy, but Bertorelli's was a second home. For two years we ate there – sometimes twice a day. It was cheap, crowded and cheerful. Lily, the Junoesque waitress, was friendly and swift, there were occasional celebrities to goggle at – Antonia White, David Jones, Nina Hamnett, Wyndham Lewis – and always plenty of friends. (In later years Nina used to relate how, when hard up, she hawked, for a few bob each, a parcel of Modigliani drawings round Bertorelli's without a single sale. Would I have bought one then? I wonder. It's difficult to look seriously at what is offered at a café table.)

Bertorelli's, started in 1913, is still a family firm. One of the founders, Giuseppe, was still alive in 1982, and the grandchildren still run the chain of excellent restaurants that bears their name. Bertorelli's has not changed and – at the south end at least – Charlotte Street still keeps its self-respecting, early-Victorian air – sooty brickwork, rickety sash windows, crooked chimney pots, dozing cats, European accents. The artists (Sickert, Whistler and Richard Wilson once lived hereabouts) seem to have gone but the strip clubs and amusement arcades have luckily not yet crossed Oxford Street. Charlotte Street keeps to basics – food, drink, tobacco, hardware. Quick turnover, small profits, family staff – unpretentious, industrious, self-reliant.

The Debenham House – 8 Addison Road

A wide, sun-filled road lined with vast Italianate villas and smaller Victorian terrace houses dozing away behind crooked brick walls and important gate piers. It might be Cheltenham or Hove. Here at No 13 in the gentle misty setting of Art Workers' Guild furnishings lived M's tiny, iron-willed aunt – daughter of George MacDonald – and her husband Edward – a retired Permanent Secretary of liberal views, with a black-ribboned pince-nez, large friendly teeth, carefully combed white hair. In her college holidays M would sometimes lodge there for a week or so and I was a visitor for tea. A tiny blue flame flickered under the silver kettle, somebody played the piano. Photograph albums were leafed through. The garden was shown.

To reach this experience I had to pass No 8 – surely still one of the most extraordinary houses in London. It was built in 1907 for Sir Ernest Debenham the draper. The architect was Halsey Ricardo – then about sixty years old – the Rugby-educated son of a banker and rich enough to be choosy in his commissions. Early in his career he became obsessed with the drabness and lack of colour in England's architecture – 'We have tried mass and form, light and shade', he wrote, 'might we not now try colour?' He tried it here with spectacular results . . . pink, cream terracotta, green and blue. Every surface is moulded, glazed and brightly coloured . . . Burmanstoft's Staffordshire bricks, Doulton's tile. The inside is equally splendid, much of the designs and furnishings being provided by fellow-members of the Art Workers' Guild – De Morgan tiles (some of them saved from a series designed for the Tzar's yacht *Lividia*), Gimson ceilings, Aumonier woodwork, E.S. Prior stained glass. How nice, in these sticky, self-conscious days, to see such apparently effortless and amiable collaboration. No heart-searching seminars. No Arts Council prodding. Just mutual respect for each other's craft, a determination to contribute worthily, but always a willingness to be part of a whole . . . and I suppose a lot of money to pay for it all.

But wealth can be also a stifler of talent and sadly for us Ricardo – a prolific writer – built little else that has survived. (The splendid Howrah Station in Calcutta is out of sight for most people.) But here, displayed like a peacock tail among the luxurious shrubberies of West Kensington (to quote Gaetano, Sir William Richmond's assistant on the mosaics of St Paul's), here he certainly 'superseded himself' . . . and thanks to the quality of the work and to the care of subsequent owners, it glows and glitters as brightly as ever for our enjoyment.

8 Addison Road W. 14.

The Albert Memorial

Prince Albert died in 1861. 'We have lost him', wrote Lord Tennyson, the Poet Laureate, 'he is gone . . . all narrow jealousies are silent and we see him as he moved . . . how modest, kindly, all accomplished . . . wise . . . noble father of the Kings to be.' After a moment's shocked paralysis the country sprang into action. The Victorians were enjoyably addicted to death, funerals, eulogies and memorials, and here was richness indeed. All over the land 'narrow jealousies' flickered like summer lightning above the heads of bigwigs and busybodies forming committees, collecting money, debating ideas. Sculptors secretly rubbed their hands. Dyers worked overtime. Music shops ran out of requiem scores.

The first proposal for London – a giant obelisk of granite – failed to find royal favour and in the end a limited competition was mounted. It was won by Sir Gilbert Scott, with the only Gothic-style entry to be submitted. His design, half-jewellery half-architecture – polychromatic, richly emblazoned, glittering with mosaic, enamel, marble and granite – was conceived as a shrine. Within this richness, like a Buddha in a Bangkok pagoda, sits the giant, once-gilded figure of Prince Albert, a handsome work by Foley, flanked by sculptures each by a different sculptor depicting Agriculture, Engineering, Manufactures and Commerce. On the perimeter of the podium stand the marble outriders of Europe, Asia, Africa and the Americas, and room was found, too, for the figures of Faith, Hope, Charity, Humility, Fortitude, Prudence and Justice, while beneath, where Albert sits reading the catalogue of the 1851 Exhibition, marches a frieze of the world's greatest artists. (Imagine the hours of committee debate deciding who to include. Scott is there but with his back to us.) The contractors built it free and when the memorial was nearing completion, Sir Gilbert gave a party – beef, plum pudding and cheese – for the 80 workmen, most of them teetotallers, in recognition of their skill and their forbearance from bad language on the scaffold.

As a memorial it fails completely to touch the heart. Other peoples' virtues and possessions so solidly celebrated are chilly companions, but its earnest spikiness in the end pierces one's initial resistance and it is always fun to explore the sculpture and guess at the identities. Although much criticised on completion (1872) and treated as a joke by my parents' generation, it still keeps its jewelled grip on the public's affection and is never without its idly perambulating circle of admirers. The permanent priestesses of this shrine, as I could observe from my Royal College of Art office, are the posh nannies of Kensington who, sternly uniformed and protected by a laager of coronetted prams, gathered there each afternoon to exchange gossip about their charges and employers.

Gilbert Scott successfully fought off the critics and on its completion was rewarded with a knighthood by his grateful sovereign. Those interested in statistics may wish to learn that it is 175 feet high and cost £120,000.

Albert Memorial

AL.

Old Church St. Chelsea.

— the two houses on the left
are by Walter Gropius & Max Fry
and by Erich Mendelsohn &
Serge Chermayeff. — Both built
1936.

From January to May 1940 we
lodged on the ground floor of
this little stuccoed dolls-house
on the West side of
Old Church St.

Old Church Street, Chelsea

A tiny Jewish cemetery and a famous artists' pub of the 'fifties, 'The Queen's Elm', guard the Fulham Road entrance. From here Old Church Street – like all good streets – curves gently away out of sight. It crosses the King's Road, narrows to alley-width before exploding on to the Embankment (built 1874) by All Saints' Church, (rebuilt after the war), and finally reaches the distant glitter of the tideway.

On the east side it is almost entirely new housettes in Chelsea Georgette style (Bunce's little Dairy vanished in the Blitz), but the west side is still a pleasantly rich assortment of stucco façades, plum-coloured garden walls, and eagle-topped gate piers concealing leafy gardens. One of the smallest of the houses, No 12, wedged like a tiny monograph between encyclopedias, is where, when first married, we rented rooms until driven out by the air-raids of 1940.

For six happy years between 1933 and 1939 I enjoyed the view of this street every working day of my life, for it lay beneath the window of the one-room office over a chemist's shop which I shared, first as an assistant and later as partner with Christopher Nicholson. (How pleased we were when Gropius and Mendelssohn, with their English partners, built here, opposite the dolls-house-size Chelsea Arts Club, and before our very eyes, two white flat-roofed houses, that became ikons of the Modern Movement.)

Our practice was as modest as our office – mostly conversions for friends and relations. Kit Nicholson – tragically killed after the war in a gliding accident – was a fine and serious architect and always the liveliest of company. We both of us enjoyed regular visits from his father – the painter William – an entertainingly dapper figure wearing a spotted shirt, patent leather shoes and a tiny pork-pie hat, who once arrived triumphantly waving an envelope addressed to him c/o The Royal Academy and readdressed 'Not known here'. Through him and his beloved crony, Edwin Lutyens, we took on some work for Edward James, a delightful and alarmingly elegant young man busy at the time launching into London his protégé Salvador Dali. With both of them we worked on James's house in Wimpole Street (where rested the famous Mae West-lips sofa) and, at Monkton House, a Sussex shooting-box which we helped transform into a fantasy of draped chimneys and palm tree columns. Dali, who worked hard but with evident enjoyment at his role as a professional 'provocateur' ('It's hard', he used to sigh, 'to keep the world's attention for more than half-an-hour') kept us busy, if unsuccessfully, trying to realise his more elaborate projects – life-size exploding swans, rooms that 'breathed' irregularly like sick dogs, huge clocks that displayed different (Dali-mixed) colours for every day of the week – until the war brought it all to an end and the office was closed for the duration

Mary Ward Settlement

In 1895 a competition was held for a charitable building in Bloomsbury. It was assessed by Norman Shaw – one could almost say as usual – and was won by two young architects Dunbar Smith and a cousin of M's, Cecil Brewer. It met with a guarded welcome from the professional press but its Voyseyesqe style – deeply overhanging eaves, lots of white paint and red brick spreading easily from the moulded stone doorway – proved influential, particularly in the LCC architect's department. (Traces of the door reappear in Macintosh's famous Glasgow Art School a year later and in the Public Library at Gosport.) Smith was a student at the Royal Academy Schools and the Mary Ward Settlement was their first big job. (Better known perhaps are Heal's Store in Tottenham Court Road and the National Museum of Wales, Cardiff.) Nevertheless, the Settlement is a remarkable and original building – appropriately friendly with a touch of do-goodery in its steady gaze at the passers-by.

Hampton Court

The sights of London for most of us tend to vanish with the family push-chairs. No more Sunday trips to Richmond or Greenwich or Bethnal Green until the grandchildren arrive for 'Round Two'. Hampton Court is one of those places where (to quote Logan Pearsall Smith) 'I am found more often in the spirit than in the flesh . . .' perhaps because it is too vast, too famous, too rambling, too packed with pictures, too enmeshed with history to be comfortably faced. It helps a little to remember the principal actors on this flamboyant stage.

First Cardinal Wolsey, Lord Chancellor to Henry VIII, who bought the site – believing it to be a healthy one – began the Tudor Palace with its forest of chimneys and sequence of courtyards and then, thinking he was in danger of incurring royal displeasure by such grandeur (his household numbered over 500 persons), presented it in 1525 to his Sovereign. It did not save him. Next Henry VIII who rebuilt the Great Hall and enlarged the Wolsey Palace with apartments later to be demolished. (Anne Boleyn's cipher 'A.B.' survives in the Great Hall but was altered in 1536 to read 'J.S.' for Jane Seymour. Only the last of his Queens, Catherine Parr, lived to enjoy Hampton Court where she was married.)

Charles I was imprisoned here. Charles II laid out the avenues and canals of the Home Park. William and Mary decided to live here in a greatly enlarged palace designed by Christopher Wren (whose first plan was to demolish everything and rebuild). The rooms of King William, both state and private, looked south to the river, those of Queen Mary east over the Park. They met so to speak on the south-east corner, first floor. George I and George II made further alterations and additions, but George III never lived here and in 1838 Queen Victoria opened it all to the public.

So much for the actors . . . what of the scenery?

There's plenty to see – roses and cherubs, tapestries, paintings, armour, cartoons, murals, scrolls and enrichments in plaster and iron. But Hampton Court manages to keep human in scale and personal in flavour. More like an Oxbridge College than a Royal Palace – inconsequently arranged, stylistically inconsistent, it is unified by the material of which it is built . . . a brick – rose, lilac, cherry-red, orange in colour – that looks as if it had stored the day's sunshine and would still be warm to the touch. Look out for the astronomical clock marking high water at London Bridge – Hampton Court was built as a riverside palace – the Tudor portraits, Lely's ladies and the fantastically elaborate Chapel.

Hampton Court Palace.

H2.

St Margaret's Westminster
sidling up to the shadowy flank
of the Abbey looks like a
tug fussing round a liner.
Mostly 16th C with a pretty
18th C Gothic tower by John
James — all much restored.
Famous between the wars
for the smartest weddings...
& occasionally for modest ones.
In 1938 M & I were married
here as the guests of the
Rector, Canon Storr, an
old friend of my father-in-law —
to do justice to such unexpected
glory — church, choir, bells, the lot...
we surrounded ourselves with
all friends available &
had a really splendid day.

The Boat House Syon.
for ten years the home of Robin Darwin ...

PART TWO

the scene of many family picnics.

Protected from the car parks and supermarkets of Brentford by a huge wandering brick wall the colour of mulberries lies Syon ... the last great-house in London still privately owned ... Grounds by Capability Brown, magnificent glass-houses by Fowler (1827). a deadpan face concealing one of the most spectacular interiors in Europe.

Syon House

Across the river but not far away is Isleworth – another of Turner's hideaways – watched over by the last great private palace in London, Syon House, four-square and deadpan in its setting of watermeadows and cedar trees. Syon was given to the Earl of Northumberland, father-in-law of Lady Jane Grey, in 1553. From Syon she went to the Tower to be proclaimed Queen, and later to be beheaded – as indeed was her father-in-law. In 1594 the house reverted to the Northumberland family who have lived there ever since. The flat, uncommunicative façade – it looks as if it was built of cardboard – gives no hint of the glories within. And glories they are. In 1761 the interior of the house was transformed by Robert Adam. 'The idea,' wrote Adam excitedly, 'was a favourite one and the money unlimited.' To walk through this sequence of great rooms – hall, ante-room, dining room, drawing room, long gallery, all gilded, corniced, painted and delicately adorned – 'as superb', wrote Sacheverell Sitwell, 'as any Roman interior in the palaces of the Caesars', is to experience one of the great architectural journeys of England, and one easily arranged, for the house, the grounds – begun in the sixteenth century – and the magnificent domed glasshouses by Charles Fowler (1827), are all normally open to the public.

South Bank

Water again. This time the Thames between Westminster and Waterloo Bridges. It was 1948. From my office as the newly appointed Director of Architecture for the Festival of Britain, I could enjoy a sideways glimpse of Admiral's Reach and the South Bank – then a derelict area of broken bricks, collapsed wharves, and greasy mudflats. Miraculously there was one tree which had survived (still there) but no buildings except the old Shot Tower, working and in the charge of two old men who, unspeaking and mutually dependent, moved about their tasks like a couple of fishermen in a boat.

It was our task in the Festival Office to transform this unpromising battlefield into an exhibition designed, so said the brief, to celebrate the history, achievement and future promise of Britain. We had three years to prepare and build it. It was not an auspicious moment. There was war in Korea. Rationing was stricter than in wartime. Everybody was in a tired and scratchy mood. To many people the Festival, conceived by its inventor Gerald Barry as a tonic to the nation, seemed more like a lollipop stuck into our mouths to keep us quiet. The press was universally hostile. Conservatives suspected it as a smokescreen for advancing Socialism. Labour dismissed it as a typical piece of middle-class cultural colonialism. Luckily we were too busy to listen for the catcalls and in the end, despite strikes, shortages and appalling weather, the South Bank exhibition – light-hearted, multi-coloured, in place a bit cute perhaps, serious without being solemn – opened on time within reach of its budget and proved a huge success.

Only the Embankment, the Festival Hall and that tree survive among the exhibition's flat-faced, flat-footed successors. One of the triumphs of the South Bank was the North Bank – a great backdrop of buildings from the Palace of Westminster to the Savoy Hotel, seen almost for the first time. Most spectacular of these – it was honoured by being placed on the axis of the exhibition's fairway – was Whitehall Court, a Victorian Camelot of turrets and spires designed in 1884 by Archer and Shee (the National Liberal Club at the east end is by Waterhouse), architects of the similarly splendid Hyde Park Hotel. The principal promoter of both was a stout, florid and bearded non-conformist called Jabez Balfour, who masterminded an ingenious, complicated and fraudulent financial web – Albert Hall Mansions was another of his enterprises – in which he and his partners became eventually trapped. There was a public outcry, his properties were auctioned off. Balfour fled to South America, was brought back for trial and sentenced to fourteen years. He died in 1916 in a railway carriage just outside Reading. Rascal he may have been but he was an enterprising patron and it is difficult not to think gratefully of a man who so enriched the London skyline.

The Royal Albert Hall

For twenty years or so from my office on the top corner of the Royal College of Art I looked down upon the shiny tin pate of the Royal Albert Hall, watching the punters surge in and out . . . limousined members of the Institute of Directors or boxing fans on foot, Women's Institute (a flowerbed of hats), young promenaders and Girl-Guides, potential Miss Worlds glassy-eyed in their coach, Wagner-lovers, table-tennis buffs or capped and gowned students. Down the great red hatch they all went later to be disgorged into the lamplit dark. Like some portly, red-faced old uncle, the Albert Hall seemed to welcome them all with equal warmth. No wonder that for all its faults we love it. No wonder it has escaped the ups and downs of taste suffered by its neighbour across the road.

The Albert Hall looks solid enough but it had a rocky start. Thought up by Henry Cole (the impresario of the Crystal Palace) on outrageously ambitious lines (30,000 seats), it floundered about for years until 1861 and the death of Prince Albert. Surely, thought Cole (who, like all good Victorians, loved a pious cause from which money could be made), this sad event could be turned to good account. And so it proved, though subscriptions at first were embarrassingly slow to come in. Something smaller, cheaper and easier to finance had to be devised, and the final concept – 6,000 seats round a central amphitheatre, a girdle of corridors and an outer ring of lavatories, offices and buffet bars, all mounted on a substructure of store and service rooms – was sensible and convenient. Henry Willis was commissioned to design the largest organ in the world. The foundation stone was laid in March 1867 and four years later the Prince of Wales – his mother was too moved to speak – declared it open. The early years proved to be a nightmare of difficulties. The hall wasn't quite finished, it had developed a nasty echo, public response to concerts was discouraging. Arguments with the seat-holder subscribers flickered like distant fireworks for year after year. More money was pumped in, activities in arts and sciences (the main purpose of the hall) became now stretched to include more popular exhibitions and dances, and eventually film shows, political meetings, Japanese wrestlers and boxing. After the First World War – non-stop renderings it seemed by Dame Clara Butt of 'Land of Hope and Glory' – there were beauty contests and motor shows, roller-skating, celebrity concerts and the first links with the BBC. Reopened (undamaged) after the Second World War it became the new home of the Proms.

In 1970, M and I were lucky enough to be asked to advise upon its total redecoration (the auditorium was previously decorated in cream, red and Cambridge blue) and we got to know and love every part of it, and to appreciate also the practicalities of the problem – beer-crates in the boxes on boxing night, chewing gum on the carpets on pop nights, inaccessible light points and leaky roofs. When finished the results were shown to and approved by the Promenaders, so all was well.

What is the secret of its bouncing success? First its look of permanence. It is as dependable-looking as a pillar box. Second its accessibility to every interest and every age of audience. Third – thanks to Cole, and to Fowke and Scott the Royal Engineer designers – its enveloping form that sweeps everybody up so that we are all part of what is going on.

Thurloe Place, South Kensington

For me Thurloe Place, South Kensington, is a real home patch. The two-storey
building on the left has been for thirty years the cosily crowded office of our
architectural practice. (The Cockade sign over the door is a relic of the immediate
post-war days when the place was occupied by a design firm for which my wife and
I both worked.) Just out of sight to the left is No 21–23 Cromwell Road, an outpost
of the Royal College of Art, containing in the 1960s the Common Rooms, Library
and my own department of Interior Design. The blue-and-white building beyond is
the recently completed Ismaili Centre, designed by my partners for the Aga Khan's
London community. (The site was originally designated for the National Theatre.)
The elaborate tower beyond belongs to the Victoria & Albert Museum, a clumsy
and over-cooked building built around 1900 in what has been termed a confused
Renaissance style to the design of Aston Webb. (He won the competition assessed by
Alfred Waterhouse.) It's a fine museum to visit but can be no fun at all to run –
rambling, multi-levelled, inconsequential. Don't miss the magnificently restored
Minton-tiled tea rooms: not easy to find but well worth the trip. The museum's
scarlet, congested face stares across Cromwell Road at Thurloe Square, built in 1839,
and the grandest of the local developments masterminded for the Thurloe-Alexander
families by George Basevi – pupil of Sir John Soane.

The proximity of the Great Exhibition site and gardens to the north helped the
estate to prosper and the arrival of the District Railway in 1868 set the seal on its
success as a local 'village centre', small in scale, decently unpretentious, sheltered from
the surge of traffic that sweeps as regularly as the tide along Cromwell Road by a
stuccoed cliff of terraced mansions that march westwards in relentless, heavy-footed
unison. Thurloe Place to me is more than a charming but unremarkable little
side-street. It is a monument to a vow made way back in the 'thirties to work, if I
could afford it, within walking distance of where I lived. For nearly fifty years we
managed it. We preferred anyway the professionally unfashionable areas of Fulham
and Old Brompton Road to Bloomsbury and the West End.

Today, architects, quite rightly, work from anywhere they find comfortable –
Smithfield or Wandsworth, Highbury or Barnes – in disused tramsheds and converted
launderettes or attic bedsitters, contributing no doubt, with such enterprise and sense,
to the slow death of the inner city. No wonder. For who would seriously enjoy
(except those only impressed by labels and engraved writing paper), given the chance,
to work (much less live) among the car-showrooms, pizza parlours and shoe-shops of
Westminster and Holborn? A century ago St James's Street and Park Lane were the
twin poles around which society self-admiringly revolved. Twenty years ago Eaton
Square was perhaps the maypole round which danced the rich and the ambitious.
Today perhaps the Boltons or even further. Chic – radical or otherwise – is always
on the move and in most cities it goes west.

Holland House Park

In 1940, Holland House, the last great country mansion to remain in central London, was burnt to the ground by an incendiary bomb. (Luckily most of the contents had been previously removed to the country.) In 1951 the house and grounds were acquired by the LCC and not long afterwards we were asked to design a Youth Hostel as an extension to the roofless east wing, while repairs to what was left of the old house were undertaken by the LCC. It was a fascinating and difficult assignment. The entrance court was turfed over and separated from the old house by a moat, and watched over by the new block painted inconspicuously sludge-green and white – the whole composition anchored by brick garden walls. The old house was Jacobean but looked Victorian – partly designed by John Thorpe about 1695 for Sir Walter Cope and afterwards almost continuously altered up to the nineteenth century. Its social career was brilliant. In the eighteenth and nineteenth centuries Holland House was the centre of Whig society and the home of the remarkable Fox family. Virtually everybody of note was a visitor – Addison, Joshua Reynolds, Wordsworth, Walter Scott, Sydney Smith – and in later years during its second flowering, Dumas and Talleyrand and finally G.F. Watts, the dazzling young painter protégé of Lady Holland – 'He came to stay at little Holland House for three days and stayed for thirty years.' Here was another centre – Tennyson, Burne-Jones, Thackeray, Rossetti, Gladstone and Disraeli. Watts moved to Melbury Road and then to Compton near Guildford, cossetted throughout his life by a series of devoted married ladies who handed him – a secretive, melancholy, self-obsessed, prosy puritan – from one to the other like a baton.

At the end of the war the gardens, like the house, were in ruins. Today they have been beautifully and inconspicuously restored and, despite weekend crowds, still look private and sequestered. Peacocks strut, rabbits nibble, squirrels stare. The early nineteenth-century garden ballroom is now a restaurant, the orangery a place to sit out of the wind, an imaginatively designed children's playground swarms with happy tots. It could hardly have been done better.

Tower Bridge

Asked to nominate a building that epitomises in its architecture the attitudes and achievements of the Victorian age – technical daring, entrepreneurial confidence, richness of detail – you'd find it difficult to beat Tower Bridge. (Runner-up? Perhaps St Pancras.) A new bridge had been needed here for years and in 1885 the decision was taken to provide one. It was a difficult problem. It had to be high enough to permit the passage of largish vessels but there was no room (as with New York's Brooklyn Bridge) to provide the necessary approach ramps. The solution – half-suspension bridge, half-drawbridge, crowned with Gothic turrets – was the combined work of an architect and an engineer – Sir Horace Jones, the jolly, globular Freemason son of a solicitor, and John Wolfe Barry, son of Sir Charles and an expert on railways. Both must share the honours. Appointed City architect in 1864 after a few years in private practice (Cardiff Town Hall and Marshall & Snelgrove) Horace Jones had been busy with the City Markets of Leadenhall, Billingsgate and Smithfield – not to mention the Guildhall School of Music and the City Lunatic Asylum. Barry had been assistant to Hawkshaw on Charing Cross and Cannon Street stations.

Technically Tower Bridge was adventurous. The two bascules, counterbalanced and pivoted and operated by hydraulic machinery, share the centre span of 200 feet. The side spans are suspended. Two pinnacled towers – the work largely of Horace Jones who died before their completion – carry a high-level walkway reached by lifts. To watch the roadway rise slowly, to wait for the first bits of straw and paper to begin their trickle down the gradually sloping gutters, was a childhood delight seldom nowadays to be enjoyed, but the splendid engine rooms are on public show and Tower Bridge is still one of the most popular sights of London . . . and one of the most romantic. In her book on Victorian London, Priscilla Metcalfe claims that Charles Barry's Palace of Westminster is really the first great 'Victorian' building, just as Tower Bridge – designed in part by Barry's son – is the last. She is right. Between these two romantic silhouettes softened by the river mist lies nineteenth-century London – less grandly dim because the air is clear of smoke, less deafeningly clamorous because no iron-clad wheels crash over the cobbles, but still an image to be recognised.

Buckingham Palace

Like Dartmoor Prison gazed at daily across the stony hills by tourists, the main façade of Buckingham Palace gives nothing away. Silent behind its flat pilasters and curtained windows, it gazes unmoved at the elaborate marble explosion of the Victoria Memorial which blocks its view of the Mall. It seems behind its massive railings as remote, deadpan and mysterious as a Tibetan monastery. Only glimpses – the flick of the Royal Standard, a housemaid's face at a window, a footman sighted at a scarlet-carpeted side-door – show that it is occupied and that, behind the façade, designed in 1913 by Sir Aston Webb and rushed up in three months to meet an instruction from George V, is a rambling palace of an internal complexity and richness that rivals the history of its building.

Although since Queen Victoria's day the official residence of the Sovereign, it was not built as such. The original house (1705) was bought by George III in 1762 as a London *pied à terre*. Forty years later George IV, having outgrown his opulent and continually expanding Carlton House home given him on his twenty-first birthday – 'a tawdry, childish place' said *The Times* – decided to make of Buckingham House a proper palace. Sir John Soane hoped for the job – had indeed produced a palace design on spec – but the commission went to John Nash. Nash, a snobbish, snub-nosed and adventurous property speculator and architect, was then at the peak of his fame with many royal commissions at Brighton, Carlton House, Regent's Park and Windsor already behind him or in hand. Born in London he had set up in Wales as a speculative builder, gone predictably bankrupt and then joined up with Humphrey Repton, the landscape architect – from whom no doubt he learned his astonishing mastery of scale and spatial playfulness. Indeed the most famous bits of London – Regent's Park, Regent Street, Carlton House Terrace, Haymarket Theatre, Trafalgar Square – are his work. But his royal connections (strengthened, it was said, by taking on as his wife a discarded royal mistress) could not save him from disaster and Buckingham Palace proved to be his downfall.

Not for the first time he found he had two masters to please – the Prince Regent and the Government, each with conflicting orders. Costs mounted, at the same rate as public criticism. Eventually there was a showdown, charges of professional incompetence, hideous design – his central dome was described as an upturned slop-pail – and financial jobbery (providing bricks from his own brickfield). Nash was dismissed, the Duke of Wellington refused him a baronetcy, and he retired to the Isle of Wight to die in debt and in disgrace.

Externally only the West façade – facing the gardens – remains recognisably Nash's work. His Marble Arch (placed in the quadrangle facing the Mall) was removed to its present home. The remodelling of Windsor Castle was entrusted to

James Wyatt and Joseph Pennethorne, and Edward Blore was hired to complete Buckingham Palace. The house is built around a pinkly-sanded central courtyard. The North wing houses the first-floor private apartments above offices. The East wing (facing the Mall) and West wing (facing the gardens) contains State guest and reception rooms. The South wing has more offices and staff quarters. The garden front is the prettiest – pale stone, white sash windows balanced round a central curving bay – more like a terrace of houses than a palace. In the gardens, picturesquely planned by W.T. Aiton, huge trees stand in the pools of their shadows, and the lawns slope down to the lake where flamingoes mince through the shallows.

St John's Smith Square

The eighteenth-century church of St John's Smith Square is one of London's secret masterpieces. Secret because although almost in the shadow of Big Ben it is not easy to find. (Indeed I had never set eyes on it myself until commissioned in 1946 to draw it as a bombed-out ruin.) Not everybody admires it – for it is an odd-looking building. (It's been called 'absurd', 'wretched' and 'hideous'. Dickens thought it was 'frightful'.) It is squarish in plan, heavy in form, its external walls alive and ponderously flickering with cornices, columns and pediments, the whole pulsating composition pegged to the ground with four heavily modelled towers. It dominates – almost bullies – the quiet, leafy square in which it sits like some monster piece of abandoned machinery. Inside it comes to a stop – quiet, simple, lofty and dignified – white walls, dark wood, scarlet hangings. Don't miss the crypt. It's tremendous, a Piranesi interior of low brick vaulting bearing, it seems, the weight of the world upon its arches.

The architect was Thomas Archer, a well-born, wealthy and popular country gentleman with an appointment at Court and not therefore professionally very prolific. (He designed Birmingham Cathedral and St Paul's Deptford.) It took a long time to build – from 1713 to 1728 – for there were structural problems. The site was marshy and the church began to sink and the towers had to be redesigned and lightened. It cost £40,875. It was to enjoy an eventful life. In 1742 it was destroyed by fire, in 1773 struck by lightning, in 1815 the towers had again to be strengthened, in 1941 it was gutted by a fire bomb and for twenty years it stood empty to the sky. Between 1965–9 it was rebuilt to begin its new successful career as a concert hall – for me almost my favourite in London.

Chiswick Mall

At one time London used to end officially at Hammersmith Bridge . . . and you might think so still. Trees, towpaths, mudflats still line the river banks and the eighteenth- and nineteenth-century houses of Chiswick Reach, ranged behind their garden walls, look no more imposing than a village street.

After we had moved to London in 1946, it became a popular family walk for Sundays, and in later years many of our friends drifted upriver to live hereabouts. Not surprising, for the water, whether darkening ahead of wind-squalls or shiny-flat as a pewter plate, is always alive with activity, and through open windows you can see light patterns reflected from the water dancing on the ceilings.

The buildings get posher as you walk upstream from the Bridge – first the pubs and boathouses, the industrial relics and municipal benches. Then straight-faced Kelmscott House, once the house of William Morris and George MacDonald, where one afternoon in 1872 John Ruskin was for a few hours reunited in passionate misery with his child-love Rose la Touche. Next the high, cramped formality of Hammersmith Terrace where the road side-steps briefly inland, a discreetly designed group of studios, some absurd Beggar's Opera maisonettes, a pretty row of seventeenth–nineteenth-century houses drenched in forsythia, where once lived Beerbohm Tree and Nigel Playfair (and many actors and artists since), the house of Barbara Villiers who had five children by Charles II and died of smallpox, the draw dock where timber and coal and malt were brought for the brewery, larger and grander houses, and finally, at the corner of Church Street wriggling inland, the Parish Church of St Nicholas – Victorian except for its fifteenth-century tower – where are buried Burlington, Whistler, Kent and Hogarth, the wording of whose epitaph, written by Garrick, was so sharply criticised by Dr Johnson.

At the top of Church Street – lined with Beatrix Potter-scale cottages – and across the roaring motorway stands Burlington's Chiswick House, a hard-edged manifesto in stone of Burlington's Palladian principles – formal without, more exuberant within, penned in its arcadian setting of lakes and follies and lawns upon which Hogarth's house by the garden wall turns its disapproving back. It was designed (1725–29) largely by Burlington himself, but with Kent's help, to house his collection of pictures and antiquities. The extensions designed later by Wyatt have since been demolished. Today it is a peaceful, often deserted place. Who could believe that from the foot of Church Street in this setting of a nobleman's park and clustering cottages, was launched on 18 May 1893, from John Thorneycroft's tiny yard, the three-funnelled 27-knot torpedo gunboat HMS *Speedy*?

There has been a church here by the river for over 500 years. St Mary's — the present parish church — was built 1775/7 by Joseph Dixon.

The steps of the pillared porch looking up-river makes one of the sunniest & nicest places to sit in all London.

Leighton House
(overleaf)

Not to be missed by connoisseurs of vanished glories. I came across it shamefully late in life when exploring the ruins of Holland House in the last year of the war. It stands on the edge of Holland Park, just off Melbury Road which, a century ago, was the Beverley Hills of the art world, where lived artists like Fildes, Watts, Marcus Stone, and Burges – a man so childlike in appearance that Rossetti always felt like offering him a bullseye. No pavement café Bohemia here. Receptions, rather, and carriages, menservants, leisurely travel, the smell of cigars and toilet water. Industrious, rich, successful and self-satisfied, the artists lived as grandly as movie moguls – which, given the chance, some of them, for example Orchardson, might easily have been. These were the days, remember, when the engraving profits from a single picture were high enough to get yourself a splendid mansion by your Royal Academy colleague Norman Shaw. (No wonder Luke Fildes could afford a full-size mock-up of a crofter's cottage in his studio in which to paint 'The Doctor'.)

Zeus of this red-brick and sash-windowed Olympia was Frederick Leighton, grandson of the Tsar's physician, a traveller, scholar, linguist, the President of the Royal Academy from 1878–96, the golden years of its unchallenged power. Handsome, precise, stately in movement (though a lively dancer), punctilious in his duties, simple in his personal life, he was a never-to-be-measured paragon of presidential virtues. He was a good horseman and, like his predecessor, Sir Francis Grant, neither drank nor smoked in public. He was generous to the hard-up, polite to critics. No hint of sex disturbed the classic serenity of his ivory-fleshed nudes. After he died, loaded with honours, he lay in state at Burlington House, was buried in St Paul's Cathedral and mourned by thousands who lined the streets. Dutiful to the very end, his last words were 'Give my love to the Royal Academy'.

The house he had had designed for him in Holland Park Road nearby, by his old student friend George Aitchison (the surveyor of Tooting), was a perfect monument to his character and taste . . . a tiny and austerely equipped personal flat, two huge studios (one for winter the other for summer light), a ritualistic sequence of rooms for entertaining and back stairs for models and dealers (he never discussed prices except through his manservant) and the 'chef d'oeuvre' – the two-storeyed Arab Hall – a jewelled casket of a room tiled and ornamented in the Moorish manner by his friends Walter Crane, Caldecott and Boehm. Deadpan without and exotic within, owned and cared for now by the Royal Borough of Kensington and Chelsea and used for modest exhibitions and occasional parties and concerts, the house was at one time intended by its owner to become the official residence of the President of the Royal Academy. That would have been an experience, but Zeus – even a dead Zeus – would have been an awe-inspiring presence . . . and what to do in the Arab Hall?

The Garden Front.
Leighton House.

Portobello Road

On Sunday morning the Portobello Road has a lie-in. No hint of Saturday's polyglot pressure-cooker that has all day packed it from wall to wall with what Wordsworth called 'the same perpetual whirl of trivial objects . . .' But on a Sunday morning Portobello Road – our local shopping street – lies as quiet as a sunstruck cat. The line of the road winding up the hill looks almost as leisurely and secluded as it once did 150 years ago when it was no more than a footpath through trees and meadows to Portobello Farm. (The name commemorates the capture by Admiral Vernon in 1739 of Puerto Bello in Mexico.) Until the 1840s there was scarcely a building throughout its length. Ten years later it was lined with shops – some of them converted from houses – the street market had become established, schools and chapels built and Portobello Farm had disappeared.

Throughout the eighteenth century Notting Hill had been covered with trees bordering on gravel pits and sloping down to the marshes where lived the gypsies, brickmakers and pig-keepers. The canal arrived in 1801, the Kensal Green Cemetery and the railway in 1830, the short-lived racecourse in 1837. For a time the railway isolated the strip of land between the line and the canal, and encouraged its separate existence as a village devoted to dog-fancying and laundry work. Rose gardens bordered the towpath and the canal itself was always busy with pleasure boats. But, as everywhere, the 'tracks' became a social boundary: to the south the respectable railway worker, to the north a rougher lot.

But if in 1840 Notting Hill was still a village with a village pump and a turnpike, glory was on the way. In 1823 Mr Ladbroke, a local landowner, commissioned an ambitious development plan from the architect and garden designer, Thomas Allason, centred upon a huge classical 'circus' one mile in diameter. It was never built but it proved to be the inspiration for this whole area of sweeping crescents, classical façades and generous communal gardens, through which Portobello Road threads its casual clamorous way. As this splendid architectural parade marched downhill to the railway it became less orderly, more ragged and ill-kempt. Today there are signs of smartening up. In terrace and square the familiar signals fly. The Japanese paper sphere dangling from the bumpy Victorian ceiling, the handwritten poster in the window announcing a local children's performance of *Noah's Fludde* (rather than *Ruddigore*), the Volvo for bearing Nicholas and Amanda off to school. Portobello Road seems to accept it all, acknowledging with a shrug the arrival of a new bookshop or, only from a distance, the classical tower of St Peter's, designed in 1857 by Thomas Allom – architect also of the spectacular Italianate towers of nearby Stanley Gardens.

Less pompous than Belgravia or Bayswater, less cute than Hampstead or Chelsea, more beautifully tree'd and stucco'd than Fulham or Wandsworth, fashionable in the eighteenth century as a summer resort, notorious in the nineteenth century for its mixture of genteel decay and appalling slums – Notting Hill is today a wonderful monument to the enterprise and imagination of four unknown and remarkable men, James Ladbroke and Charles Henry Blake, speculators, and Thomas Allason and Thomas Allom, architects. Well done them.

Euston Road Fire Station

In 1893 a new group was formed within the Architect's Department by the LCC. It was called the Housing of the Working Classes Branch. It consisted of a group of young, earnestly enthusiastic and extremely talented architects. Most of them were recently qualified students of the Architectural Association, trained in the socialist philosophy of William Morris and in the architectural language of the Arts and Crafts movement. (A similar group, also from the AA and fired with the same social consciousness and imagination, sent sparks flying in the LCC's post-war housing department in the 'fifties.) The chief architect at the turn of the century was Thomas Blashill, a modest man with a gift for spotting talent in others and for loyally backing their fancies. His team included Charlton, Fleming, Winmill and Philips – all as totally unknown still as their chief, yet each one of them an architect of outstanding quality.

Winmill, who had worked for Leonard Stokes, was a friend of Fleming and a member of the AA cycling club through which he encountered a building by Philip Webb. It was a turning-point in his life. Webb became his master. From Webb he learned the free and witty handling of oriels, gables, chimneys and porches kept within an inner discipline. He began in the Housing section working on the revolutionary design for Bethnal Green Boundary Estate, but in 1900 he was transferred to Fire Stations. His impact was immediate. The work of the LCC is by tradition anonymous but it is to Charles Winmill that this beautiful and subtly composed building of 1901 – one of the best of many excellent fire stations – can surely be attributed.

I have drawn it many times enjoying the thrust and balance of the bay windows that reflect and express the complicated plan – half-residential, half-industrial – that lies within. Not many people stop to admire it. Virtually nobody now knows the name of Winmill whose eye – said one of his foreman bricklayers – 'was like a striking hawk'.

Windsor Castle

At one time around 1,500 castles stood in England. They were built, under royal licence, by powerful individuals in order to protect and to demonstrate their power. Some were true strongholds, some were romantic visions, their dungeons empty, their ramparts used only for evening strolls. Windsor Castle is nearly 1,000 years old and has had its share of blood and terror – but not very much of it – and it is as a piece of noble scenery concealing a treasure house that we admire it today. I have worked there on and off for nearly thirty years and never tire of the way it gradually unfolds its grandeur in subtle sequence . . . the distant silhouettes across the river from Datchet, the sudden gloom of its shadow by the station, the curving, climbing High Street commanded by the great Curfew Tower, the series of gates and courtyards. Seen at any distance from any angle and in any light it never fails to catch the breath. Magical, mysterious, hopelessly romantic.

Windsor Castle consists of two courtyards separated by the Round Tower (which is not, incidentally, quite circular). The Lower Courtyard contains St George's Chapel and residential apartments. The Upper Courtyard – known as the quadrangle – is enclosed by the private and state apartments of the Sovereign. The castle was built on a chalk mound by William the Conqueror as one of the protective fortresses around London. Henry I was the first of many monarchs to live there. Edward III built St George's Chapel and rebuilt the Upper Courtyard. Elizabeth built the North Terrace, Charles II planted the Long Walk and lavished money on the state apartments (1678). A century later King George III decided to go and live there in a ground-floor bachelor suite, installing his wife and family across the quadrangle in the Victoria Tower – still the Queen's private apartments. All rooms were inconveniently *en suite*, so James Wyatville was instructed to link them with an internal gallery – some 500 feet long – above a series of service rooms, and to provide a new corner entrance and staircase. The Green, White and Crimson Drawing Rooms were redesigned, the Waterloo Chamber constructed by roofs over a courtyard and the East Terrace and gardens formed. Queen Victoria – who disliked Windsor, thinking it 'unenjoyable' – added the Grand Staircase, but the Castle as we see it today is largely the work of Wyatville. It was he who heightened the Round Tower, who crowned the Castle with battlements and towers and gave it that romantic and noble silhouette. He was the nephew of James Wyatt ('that stylistic weathercock', writes Sir John Summerson) and not nearly so clever . . . but he made of Windsor Castle a near-masterpiece.

The Palace Theatre

The Palace Theatre was the scene of one of the most unpleasant evenings of my life . . . the first disastrous night of John Osborne's *The World of Paul Slickey*, a musical fantasy starring Denis Lotis, Adrienne Corri and Marie Lohr, and directed by Kenneth Macmillan. It dealt with the adventures of a gossip columnist and involved such (for those days) rather advanced spectacles as sex-changes, a libidinous priest and a can-can with a corpse-filled coffin – all of which had been received with puzzled benevolence by the matinée audiences at Bournemouth where we had our tryout. I had done the sets. They included a newspaper office and a stately home, and were all treated as enlarged black-and-white drawings. I knew better than to attempt the costumes.

But what Bournemouth accepted London threw back at us in a bedlam of boos and jeers; not so bad for us in the wings but for those on stage a nightmare. Dispirited but contemptuous, John Osborne disappeared to Italy and I returned to architecture, if not to such extravagant examples as The Palace. It was perhaps a tiny compensation to me at least that the anticlimax to our weeks of work had occurred in such splendid surroundings. The theatre – built 1889–91 by a success-flushed Rupert D'Oyly Carte as an opera house – was technically highly advanced: it contained cantilever balconies of unprecedented dimensions, an early form of air-conditioning and an electrical switchboard claimed to be the most elaborate in existence. The architect-builder was called Holloway, but Sullivan called in Thomas Collcutt to provide the 'architecture'. Collcutt was the 'patriot architect' (as Tennyson called him) of the Imperial Institute in South Kensington – of which only the cupola'd campanile remains. It is a fine monument to the Victorian age and it was no fault of his that nobody knew quite what it was actually for. The Palace – then called the Royal English Opera House – opened on 31 June 1891 with Sir Arthur Sullivan's *Ivanhoe* but failed to attract support – and within a year owned up to what it looked like, a rather grand music hall. Pink-faced, richly attired in its Moorish Byzantine dress, it is one of London's finest theatres.

The Natural History Museum

I've always liked this charming pair of Victorian cottages (1883) nestling in the shrubberies at the corner of Cromwell Road at the feet of the Natural History Museum – surely the prettiest and most spectacular of all South Kensington's museums and arguably the best of all surviving works by Alfred Waterhouse, a north-country Quaker, compulsive sketcher and traveller, who at the time of his death (1905) was England's most famous and successful architect. For all its minor functional faults the Natural History Museum remains a masterpiece. Once again I was lucky that my office was, for nearly ten years in the 'fifties, squeezed into the old attics of a great stuccoed terrace house moored alongside Cromwell Road, so that daily I faced the Natural History Museum above the plane trees.

To climb the gently curving ramps from Cromwell Road, to pass under the moulded arches of the entrance into that Central Hall with its dizzily suspended staircase is one of the great spatial experiences of London (and as a Trustee I can often and luckily enjoy it). The long façade carries no hint of the building's tumultuous history. The idea of splitting off Natural History from the British Museum was thought up in 1861 by the brilliant, ambitious and much disliked scientist, Sir Richard Owen. He got Gladstone's support for the South Kensington site (then still occupied by exhibition buildings), designed the main concept of the plan himself and waited impatiently for money and results. In 1864 a competition was held and won by Captain Fowke (the soldier-designer of the Albert Hall) who almost immediately died. Governments came and went and it was four years before Waterhouse was asked to take over the job. Owen's plan – in sympathy with contemporary thinking – was strictly symmetrical. Fowke's design was suitably formal in plan and Renaissance in style. Waterhouse was a Gothicist, a lover of prickly silhouettes and romantically composed forms, but he owed much of his success to his tact and skill in reconciling conflicts of view. His solution was masterly: German Romanesque – symmetrical and arched windows in memory of Fowke, a picturesque silhouette, carved enrichment, modern structural methods and two-colour terra-cotta for the façades (the first time used on such a scale) met his own preferences. After the usual rows over costs, work began in 1873 and despite the bankruptcy of the contractor (Baker) the museum opened to the public in 1881 and, ever since, has proved to be a winner.

82

Marylebone Station

I once had a client who asked for her hall to be painted the colour of an October sunset shining on a Goldflake packet. This describes exactly the inflamed face of the Great Central Hotel which, clock-towered, bay-windowed and balconied, still commands the Marylebone Road without a rival in sight. Behind – 'looking', wrote Betjeman, 'like a provincial branch public library' – skulks the smallest of London's twelve termini – only three working platforms – and the last to arrive. Yet it was once the terminus of the magnificently named Grand Central Railway and the end, in every sense, of the ambitious dream of that great Victorian entrepreneur Sir Edward Watkin. Sir Edward was a cotton king who became besotted by railways. He managed the Manchester Sheffield Railway, was Chairman of the South-Eastern Railway and also of London's Metropolitan Railway . . . but the Grand Central was his favourite. He planned it as a link between Manchester and Paris. (He even started to build an Eiffel Tower at Wembley.) But the Grand Central was late in arriving (1899), the route was complicated and expensive, the rolling stock was extravagantly finished (they pioneered buffet cars with painted ceilings and stained glass) and by the time the trains reached London the cash was exhausted.

In a last thrust of extravagance, Sir Edward built the Great Central Hotel – packed to the eaves with mosaics and mirrors, marble and mahogany, stained glass and gilded columns. An orchestra played in the Palm Court, white-gloved dancers circled decorously in the Wharncliffe Ballroom. Today it is the HQ of British Rail, the setting in which, each quarter, our advisory design panel meets in the stately splendour of some ex card-room or residents' lounge. The architect was Colonel R.W. Edis – who also designed part of the Great Eastern Hotel at Liverpool Street and the ballroom at Sandringham. Edis was something of an eccentric, wore his Volunteer uniform in the office and liked a touch of theatre in his architecture as in his life. It was virtually the last of London's great railway hotels – the first had been the Great Western at Paddington (1852). In their day they rivalled in opulence and elaborate architecture the great hotels of the Canadian Pacific. Today with their uneconomically high ceilings, lincrusta dadoes and elephantine bathtaps they fight for their lives, distilling their generosity of material and robustness of finish to a world grown accustomed to bedside tea-makers and veneered chipboard.

The National Portrait Gallery

'Nobody goes to galleries', says a character in an Elizabeth Bowen novel, 'if they've anything else to do'. If true, there seem to be a lot of people with time on their hands. Attendance figures at the National Portrait Gallery, for instance, tucked gloomily away behind the National Gallery, have risen steadily in the last ten years. For a building dedicated to celebrating the British face it is surprisingly unalluring to look at – a stern and morose fugitive, it seems, from Victorian Manchester, reeking of complacent achievement. I shunned it for years, stupidly unaware of the treasures within – all the more interesting perhaps because of the splendid unevenness of their quality as works of art. Now I have had the honour and luck to be a Trustee and thus permitted backstage to join in answering the three traditional questions . . . is he (or she) worthy to be admitted, is the portrait the best available, can we afford it? I enjoy it all, though I shall never learn to love the building. It was the gift, in 1896, of William Henry Alexander: his conditions were that the Government should provide a site within $1\frac{1}{2}$ miles of St James's and that he should select the architect. He chose Ewan Christian, better known, but not much, for his churches. Christian studied galleries all over Europe and came up with a solution that is German in concept and Italian in expression. Within months of completion it was full up. A later extension (paid for by Dureen in 1933) filled equally fast, and the gallery will before long have to moved again to a new site.

It has been used to such moves. The collection was started (1856) in two floors of a house in George Street, was shifted to South Kensington and thence to Bethnal Green before sinking back with a flutter of eagle's feathers into Charing Cross Road. Its purpose is as Victorian as its façade . . . to be an example to future generations. 'I can think of no greater incentive to noble action,' wrote Lord Palmerston, 'than to see the features of those who have done things worthy of our admiration.' Well, today, money probably and sadly provides more welcome incentives than the features of the great and the good, but Palmerston was right to think there are few more fascinating interests than the study of human personality.

Here then are 8,000 'incentives' – paintings, miniatures, drawings, busts, photographs – from Elizabeth I to Beatrix Potter, Chaucer to James Joyce, Jane Austen to Princess Diana – all splendidly arranged and highly recommended.

P.S. As you leave it's worth a trip over to the traffic island bearing the statue of Nurse Cavell. At her feet is a pavement grille that reveals a subterranean passage belonging – so says a notice – to the North Thames Gas Board. Another wall notice spotted by a former Director of the National Portrait Gallery and reading 'No Smokeing' seems to have gone.

Burlington House

Not many people have the luck – as I have had for the past ten years – to work in such a grand building as this, with its columns and cornices, painted ceilings, rich plasterwork, mahogany doors built like battleships. It sounds formidable, yet buried beneath this (mostly Victorian) splendour is the simple, two-storey, plain-brick seventeenth-century house inherited in 1716 by the Earl of Burlington at the age of ten and remodelled to his advanced taste by Colen Campbell.

It was the first Palladian façade to be built in London. It may look like an institution but the atmosphere of a large private house still hangs about the reception rooms and kitchens, back stairs, cellars and attics. Parties still take place in the gilded assembly rooms and the RA schools provide, as it were, the nursery wing. This was the RA's first permanent home, reached exactly a hundred years after its foundation to provide, with royal support, a school for artists to show their work. It had been a nomadic existence: first in Pall Mall, then in Somerset House, then to the National Gallery and almost – impelled by a push from Queen Victoria – to South Kensington. This last move was successfully resisted by the then President, Francis Grant, a lazy painter but a courageous rider to hounds, who paid for his obstinacy by having his knighthood delayed. (In the end she got the last word – 'The Queen is prepared to knight Mr Grant,' she wrote, 'although she understands he boasts of never having been to Italy.')

The Government terms for the Piccadilly site – shared with other learned societies – were not ungenerous. A peppercorn rent until 2865, another storey to be added to the building to match the rest of the courtyard and new galleries to be built and maintained (at the RA's expense) over the gardens at the back. The result? A stately, rather intimidating façade that just keeps its dignity above the glittering scrum of parked cars, a suite of fine rooms – almost state apartments – used for exhibitions and meetings, a library, vaulted cellars leading to the schools and finally the great top-lit sequence of galleries, surely the finest in London, always, it seems, filled to the brim with the pale golden syrup of diffused sunlight. Here the Royal Academy – an independent, unsubsidised body governed by practising artists – runs a mixture of repertory theatre, art gallery, university and department store, and welcomes a million visitors a year.

Yet despite its stately setting – to which many member architects contributed over the years – despite its glittering Honours Board of past members – Reynolds, Constable, Gainsborough, Turner, Sargent, Stanley Spencer – its continuing record of great loan exhibitions, the opportunities it provides each year through the Summer Exhibition to thousands of practising artists, it wears its history and distinction lightly. A place run by working artists can seldom be solemn or self-satisfied for long. Plenty of rows of course (the Secretary was once knocked unconscious by a disenchanted member). Resignations – Burne Jones, Augustus John and Stanley Spencer – and

Royal Academy
Burlington House Piccadilly

later reconciliations. Absurdities – although women were from the start accepted as members, there were printed regulations about the draping of the male model when female students were present. Personal eccentricities – Sir Joshua Reynolds enjoyed a public execution; Benjamin West always wore his hat at meetings; Turner owned a pub in Wapping; the Professor of Anatomy used to circulate a plate of human brains among his students.

Those eighteenth-century pioneers would be proud of the institution they founded. Still teaching, exhibiting, watching over the interests of artists who have fallen on hard times, still riding the switchback of taste, sometimes adventurous, sometimes myopic, permanently hard-up, yet still independent and busier than it has ever been. Hip. Hip. R.A.

The Royal College of Music

Queen Victoria would have loved the view from my top-floor office at the Royal College of Art. To the left Albert seated beneath his spiky canopy; in front the Albert Hall; to the right Albert again, but this time standing up; facing him the Royal College of Music, a red-brick fairy castle, 'so like Balmoral'; and, beyond, the domed minaret of the Imperial Institute (from this viewpoint Queen Victoria could not have seen that the rest of the Institute – like the Empire itself – had gone) . . . and all as hard and shiny as a shell-case and as blood-red as a guardsman's tunic.

The Royal College of Music, where we are now working as architects, had started life first with pupils and teachers but no premises and then in Lt Cole's extraordinary sixteenth-century-style building nearby (now the Royal College of Organists). It prospered and grew. It was time to move. The 1851 Commissioners offered the site (the Albert statue occupying it had first to be removed northwards up the steps). The patronage of the Prince of Wales was obtained. Sir Samson Fox gave the money. Sir Arthur Blomfield was appointed the architect. His plan was simple and symmetrical. Administration on the ground floor, composition and theory on the first, singers and instrumentalists next, with a library in the roof. Separate staircases for men and women were provided and a Mrs Bindon was stationed in the entrance hall to see that they used them. (What happened, I wonder, at the top?) On 2 May 1894, to the sound of trumpets from the March from Gluck's *Alceste* and of a peal of bells from the Imperial Institute tower, it was opened.

It's not an easy-to-love building, too sharp-edged and rigorous. It distils an atmosphere of rectitude and prep-school vigour . . . memories of chilblained fingers following the relentless tick of the metronome . . . but the enthusiasm and warmth of staff and students, and the medley of sounds from every room, keep it humming with life, and at sunset on a fine evening it flashes a fine fire across the roofs of Kensington.

Blewcoat School

For nearly twenty years I have been a member of the Council and later also of the Executive of the National Trust. We meet every month either in Queen Anne's Gate, where there are hardly enough chairs to go round, or in the Blewcoat School, Caxton Street, where there's more room but it's not so easy to hear what people say. This is a pity because the discussions are of high quality and fascinating variety – seal-culling, tapestry repairs, blood sports, nude bathing, parking fees, planting plans, beam engines, footpath rights, fire precautions, forestry, monuments, bridges, bird sanctuaries or follies. There are always problems and every one is different. The Regional Chairmen give in turn their local reports, the experts advise – we make mistakes and usually learn from them – but the real pleasure of the meetings is that we are all generalists.

The Blewcoat School which so often harbours our debates was founded in 1688 and moved here in 1709. (It was still a school in the 1920s.) In 1954 the National Trust acquired and restored it. Nobody knows who designed it – a single panelled room above a basement, a demure exterior in brick and white-painted wood with a clock and a statue of a Bluecoat Boy in an arched niche. It is a modest home for one of the great success stories of this century.

The National Trust was born in 1894 – the three rather improbable midwives were Octavia Hill, the housing reformer, Sir Robert Hunter, a solicitor, and the Reverend Rawnsley, archaeologist and conservationist. From the start they insisted upon the freedom and flexibility of independence (there's still no Government subsidy). The Trust, now the largest private landowner in the country, looks after scores of distinguished houses, thousands of lonely acres, miles of unspoiled coastline. It boasts a million members and over five million visitors a year to the properties in its care. How appropriate that part of its cramped headquarters are contained within this unassuming little building.

Wormwood Scrubs

There's a touch of prurience about visiting a prison – or even just looking at one. It's like a vicarious encounter with a public humiliation or peering through the frosted window of a mortuary – you feel a little ashamed of being there. I discovered this some thirty years ago on my first visit to Pentonville – a stern, classically faced nineteenth-century building in North London – where a walk through the brightly lit, brightly painted cell blocks was accompanied by the menacing clang and tinkle of doors and keys and the rattle of boots on gratings. I had just become a Trustee of the Arthur Koestler Award – a generous sum donated by Arthur Koestler as a thank-offering for his release from a Spanish prison in 1937 and annually given for creative work executed in prisons – everything from pottery and composing to painting, poetry, sculpture or needlework – the BBC helping with the music side by recording the entries. Each year with the help of the Home Office the entries are assembled at some institution for assessment. M and I have served as judges for the visual arts for over twenty years, our favourite judgment seat being Kingston Prison, Portsmouth – an absurd little nursery fort complete with battlements and arrow slits and containing about one hundred 'lifers', some of whom organise the display for us and ply us with sandwiches and coffee.

But, architecturally speaking, Wormwood Scrubs – the flagship of the Prison Service – is the most spectacular – a carol service in that Lombardic-style chapel is quite an experience – a long, crouching silhouette like a Moroccan fort seen across the flats, or, as one approaches from the south, like an American armoury. The prison was built – mostly by convict labour – between 1874 and 1891 under the administrative supervision of Sir Edmund du Cane, then Chairman of the Prison Commission. The records are inconclusive but it seems likely he was also the architect. As a Major-General in the Royal Engineers he had had considerable architectural training and experience and indeed had designed the church of St Peter's on Portland in the same Lombardic style. The entrance is particularly impressive – strong yet not threatening. The medallions in the turrets are portraits of the penal reformers, Elizabeth Fry and John Howard.

Main Gateway—
Wormwood Scrubs Prison.

The Sir John Soane Museum

Undeservedly – but mercifully, perhaps, considering its size – the Soane Museum, No 13 Lincoln's Inn Fields, is one of London's less celebrated sights. It was built in 1812 next door to Soane's first London house (No 12) and was added to again (No 14) in 1824. It was designed to house a lifetime's collection of treasures including Hogarth's Election pictures and the Belzoni sarcophagus. Soane intended it to be his memorial.

John Soan (he added the 'e' later) was born in 1753, the son of a builder. He was a pupil of Dance and Holland, won medals at the Royal Academy Schools and travelled abroad. On his return he built some rather unconfident country houses and in 1788 became surveyor to the Bank of England, revealing in the Bank Stock Office a highly personal style, totally original, picturesque in essence, enlivened by ornamental grooves, segmental arches, shallow domes and secret lighting, which he refined and developed until his death in 1837. Soane seems not to have been a happy or confident man. He was tall, thin, pale, nervous, petulant and paranoiac. In middle age he inherited some money, achieved public recognition and began his collecting, and when he was sixty he began building the museum. In 1830 he catalogued its contents; in 1833 he retired and in 1837 he died and is buried in St Pancras by the monument he designed for his wife with its curious Swiss-roll ornaments.

The museum, apart from its contents, can only be described as extraordinary . . . 'detached' ceilings . . . bookcases inlaid with mirror, mirror friezes, mirror paterae, sunlight slipping furtively between wall and ceiling. For those who wish to study the handling of space and light this museum is a disturbing eye-opener.

Dulwich Art Gallery

According to Sir John Summerson, present curator of the Soane Museum, the Dulwich Art Gallery (1811–17), the first public art gallery in London, is the most individual of Sir John Soane's buildings. It was built from a curious brief. It had to include an art gallery, almshouses and a mausoleum for the benefactors. Sir Francis Bourgeois had inherited from an art-dealer friend, Desenfans, and his wife, a collection of pictures destined for a Polish national gallery. His widow supervised the building and paid for it and stipulated that the Royal Academy should keep an eye on pictures (hence my particular interest). There was hardly any money so the building is simple and understated . . . stock brick and a stone frieze and cornice. There are traces of Vanbrugh and Adam and (in the pattern of incised lines in the masonry) of Dance.

The Gallery was badly damaged during the Second World War but has now been splendidly restored. The contents are outstanding – three Rembrandts, some works by Rubens, Gainsborough, Murillo, Poussin, and some fine Dutch landscapes – but the mausoleum is the real oddity – a circular ante-chamber guarded by columns, leading into a room with the three coffins bathed in yellow light from the square cupola above, itself crowned with urns and surrounded by sarcophagi.

The Elephant House, London Zoo

The first decision of the Zoological Society founded in 1826 was not to buy an animal but to appoint an architect – Decimus Burton (only a raven's cage and a tunnel entrance remain of his work). Born, like so many similar institutions, through the energy of a few creative cranks, it is maintained by the skill and dedication of the expert and by generous, devoted and serious research, for the enjoyment of the public. It has had its share of financial dramas and eccentric administrators and beloved inmates: A.D. Bartlett, Superintendent for forty years, who stuffed Queen Victoria's pets, Frank Buckland who, as a challenge, ate a bit of every creature in his care . . . the bluebottle, he said, was the nastiest. . . . Jumbo the first elephant, Jubilee the chimp, Goldie the eagle, Guy the Gorilla, Brumas and Chi-Chi. The staff at all levels have reduced the mortality rate by 50% – animals, like many of us, mostly die from senility or self-indulgence.

What an achievement and what a delight – even if you are ambivalent about zoos – to work there for so many years as consultant . . . and an even greater delight to be able to design the new Elephant and Rhino House – in 1963. The real clients of course could not write a brief nor complain afterwards if it had been ignored, but their interpreters were strict enough. Elephants are ingenious at lock-picking, sometimes irritable, and should be protected from casual feeding. Our concept of a curving kraal of circular top-lit pens, separated by a moat from the rest of us who are kept in a twilight, executed in ribbed concrete and copper-sheathed sky-scuttles, and all set in a moated paddock, was accepted, built and occupied. On the opening day I was deluged with a trunk-full of tepid water by our chief client who then lumbered off to play with a log. Was it a compliment or a complaint?

Turner's House, Twickenham

When exploring a city it's always good advice to follow the trail of the artist. He is usually poor, so keeps clear of the smart quarters. His eye – like that of a browsing goat – is sharp and selective, spotting the street or building with character or assessing the quality of the light or the lift of a hill before settling down anywhere to live and work. Not surprisingly, many of them, like their contemporary successors, have stuck to the river and its villages – Chelsea, Chiswick, Isleworth, Twickenham and Richmond. What they enjoyed there is still discernible, though it usually has to be looked for.

Within a few hundred yards of Richmond Bridge, for instance, is Sandycombe Lane, Twickenham – a fine suburban name for a fine suburban road of red-and-white late-Victorian villas – generously be-turreted, bay-windowed and be-porched, buried in shrubs and Scots pines. Amongst them, as demure as a nursemaid at a picnic of grandees, is Sandycombe Lodge, white-stuccoed, slate-roofed, Italianate-designed and built by Turner (1813) as a home for his father and himself. (Turner had become interested in architecture through his lectures to students at the Royal Academy and enjoyed an occasional go at designing it, but this is his only surviving work.) According to contemporary descriptions the rooms were small and unpretentious, equipped with ship-models, simple earthenware dishes and two-pronged forks. The garden in those days went down to the river and kept Turner's father busy when he was not looking after his son's West End Gallery, but the river air did not suit the old man's health, and Turner, after a few years, sold the property.

The Royal Mint

It looks like an Oxford College or a regimental HQ but behind this appropriately reliable nineteenth-century façade lies the old Royal Mint – a complex of buildings round a courtyard – foundries, gold and silver melting houses, milling and annealing rooms, boiler houses, engine rooms and grinding rooms, the Pyx office and various stores and workshops. Today – now that production is moved to Wales – only offices remain.

In the eighteenth century the Royal Mint was still established uncomfortably and inefficiently in the Tower of London. It was over-staffed and under-equipped. The machinery was out-of-date, accommodation for the workers was murky, damp and unpopular . . . and anyway the space was wanted by the military. It was time to move. In 1787 a committee was set up, improvements and reforms proposed and a site chosen on Tower Hill, an old tobacco warehouse prudently within sight and cannon-range of the Tower. The site was cleared in 1804 and an architect, James Johnson, was chosen. He died after the completion of his designs and was succeeded by Robert Smirke (architect of the British Museum) who finished the building off and got all the credit for it. Not that there was much of that at the time. To us it looks handsome enough but to contemporary critics it seemed commonplace and dull – duller certainly than its contents, the great engines and furnaces installed by the engineer Rennie that thundered and glowed under the gas flares and made the ground tremble under the feet of passers-by.

The design of the medals and coins that poured from the presses was always a matter of argument. The Royal Academy was first asked to advise on how 'to perfect a coinage as a becoming work of taste and art' . . . and so was the College of Heralds. Today the advice is sought of The Royal Mint Design Advisory Committee. It meets about twice a year in the morning and in a front room at Buckingham Palace. It includes, under the chairmanship of Prince Philip, a typographer, a sculptor, an architect, a wildlife expert (birds and animals put in frequent appearances on coins and medals), a representative of the College of Arms, a poet and a numismatist. Royal Mint officials are in attendance. Discussions take place over designs and models to the thunder and crash of the Changing of the Guard in the courtyard below. The wildlife expert criticises the drawing of a paw, the Herald the relevance or accuracy of a national symbol. The glass in the tall sash windows shakes to the rhythm of the drums. It's all over in an hour and the officials return to this building at Tower Hill.

Carlton House Terrace ·

The ground floor of No 1 Carlton Gardens is the home of the Royal Fine Art Commission of which I have enjoyed being a member for over twenty years. It's always a pleasure to mount the steps by the King George VI statue and to marvel for the umpteenth time at the genius of John Nash who in under fifty years created, and organised, the series of spaces that are the delight of central London – the lakes and crescents of Regent's Park, the ball-joint of All Soul's, Langham Place, the sweep of Regent Street developing into the formality of Waterloo Place and that dramatic cascade of steps down to St James's Park between the creamy, stuccoed cliffs of Carlton House Terrace that Nash devised to replace Carlton House itself. (Being trained as a landscape architect he knew the value of mystery, concealment and surprise.) Nash was a born fixer, too – drafting leases, planning sewers and street lighting, arranging contracts – while still keeping an eye on what it all looked like. How extraordinary that in the 'thirties the Government seriously considered pulling it all down – and indeed started at the west end before they were stopped by public opinion.

Look out, at the top of the Duke of York's steps, for the tombstone of Giro, Herr Von Ribbentrop's pet dog (the German Embassy was housed in the corner building) and for the railings placed there by Mr Gladstone to prevent a repetition of the incident when he saved two ladies in a carriage from being hurled by runaway horses down the steps.

Carlton House Terraces

Olympia

The post-war years were a struggle for private architects. Building materials were licensed, housing and industry, both handled largely by national and local government, rightly had priority. Many of us scraped along by designing exhibition stands for the British Industries Fair or the Ideal Home Exhibition – virtually the only opportunities for any fun. It was fine experience and I enjoyed it tremendously – the speed, the opportunity for the witty or the unserious solution, the novelty of dealing with miniature versions of large problems, the all-night sessions (full thermos flasks and slippers were the solution for exhaustion), the all-pervading smell of size. Best of all perhaps the touch of theatre . . . everybody working for the opening day yet knowing it all would only last a few weeks.

Earl's Court and Olympia became as familiar as my own sitting room. I never took to the first – too cavernous and gloomy. But Olympia was always a delight – whether by day with the sun streaming through the great glazed roof or at night, as mysterious and dimly awesome as St Pancras. Olympia, then known as the National Agricultural Hall, opened for business on Boxing Day 1886. The architect was Henry Coe. He devised a roof span of 170 feet soaring 100 feet above the floor and it was built by the famous firm of Lucas and Son. The first exhibition was a grand circus – a Christmas tradition that lasted until 1967. In 1891 'Venice' was 'reconstructed', in 1893 'Constantinople', in 1894 'The Orient'. Soon followed trade fairs, the motor shows, the Royal Tournament, Crufts and the International Horse Show. In the First World War it was used as an Army clothing depot, in the Second as an internment centre and later as an Army stores depot, losing all its glass in the bombing. It was twice extended in the 'twenties and has lately been modernised to continue its busy life.

Sadly it's not easy to see Coe's great hall from the outside – but looking down this side-street and across the railway its sudden size and glitter provides an absurd grandeur – as if somebody had absent-mindedly left a giant Palm House in a suburban street.

18 Stafford Terrace

In a room at the top of this staircase – untouched, like the rest of this magical house, since the death of its owner, the illustrator and cartoonist Linley Sambourne – was founded the Victorian Society. The date was 25 February 1958. The hostess was the owner of the house, Lady Rosse, and Sir Nikolaus Pevsner and Sir John Betjeman were among the small group of guests invited. Tributes were paid to the pioneering taste and scholarship of Sir Kenneth Clark and the architect Goodhart-Rendel, a steering committee set up, officers elected. We had no money and no premises. Twenty-five years later, the Victorian Society is an established success . . . 3,000 members, branches and supporters in Australia and the USA, consulted and respected by national and local government, famous for its vigorous campaigning in defence of Victorian and Edwardian architecture. The wheel of taste moves at a regular speed – we can all guess what we will like next – and no doubt Victorian architecture in due course would have succeeded Regency and Georgian in public appreciation. No doubt . . . but that interest would not be so well-informed nor so active without the lively pressure of the Victorian Society. It is of course a pressure group set up to defend what is in their view worthy of defence. Their strength lies in their single-mindedness. It is for others to argue the counter-case for traffic improvement, loss of employment, better working conditions, value for money or architectural merit. The balance isn't always easy to reach and as a founder-member I have got into trouble more than once for arguing on the other side. But my admiration for the Victorian Society and their achievements remains as high as ever. No wonder they are so strong with so remarkable a birthplace. No 18 Stafford Terrace – now owned by the GLC and regularly open to the public – should not be missed by those interested to see how middle-class life was lived at the turn of the century. Everything is as it was . . . carpets and bath taps, bell-pushes and over-mantels, armchairs and wallpapers, and with the added pleasure of looking not like a museum but like a house from which the owner, top-hatted and watch-chained, has just stepped out for a stroll.

Platt's Lane, Hampstead

One of the extra pleasures of working at Westfield College, Hampstead, over the past twenty years has been catching regular sight of a delightful L-shaped house that spreads itself as comfortably as a long white cat on a sunny corner site. It was designed in 1895 for his father (then aged ninety-two) by Charles Annesley Voysey, a key figure of the Arts and Crafts movement, austere and independently minded, who evolved a style for the multitude of houses he designed so personal that he became its prisoner. He was the son of a kindly clergyman (dismissed from the Church of England for heresy), privately educated and then articled first to the Victorian architect J.F. Seddon – a Gothicist and disciple of Pugin – and then to George Devey, a prosperous designer of large country houses.

In 1882 Voysey set up his own practice and quickly established the language which was all his life to be unmistakably his. Big chimneys, huge sweeping rooves pulled down over buttressed walls – usually rough-cast – windows grouped in long horizontal bands, wide front doors – 'doors', he said, 'should suggest welcome . . . not like a coffin lid' – with heart shapes inset. Inside are low ceilings, white walls (or wallpapers of his own design), simple furniture enlivened – in his view, anyway – by an occasional jokey detail. Like the Pre-Raphaelites, the Arts and Crafts movement was riddled with an obsession for toe-curling private jokes and donnish horseplay. Occasionally Voysey broke the mould as in Sanderson's masterly little factory (1902) in Chiswick – but usually he stuck to his principles, his materials and his style.

Voysey once listed the qualities he searched for: repose, cheerfulness, simplicity, breadth, warmth, quietness in storm, economy of upkeep, evidence of protection, harmony with surroundings, absence of dark passages, evenness of temperature. Well, yes, but also I suppose a touch of middle-class high-minded smugness, a whiff of Kate Greenaway and green-painted water-butts, a schoolmasterly rigour behind it all which occasionally chills.

Voysey built over a hundred houses – there's another London beauty, Tower House in Bedford Park – every one stamped with this odd mixture of puritanism and playfulness. But though a busy man – at least until 1918 – he was never rich and he died poor (1941), still virtually unknown outside his own profession, a quiet pioneering talent that burned with a small but steady flame.

Palace of Westminster

The Palace of Westminster is a presence rather than a building, an image summoned nightly to the eye by the sound of Big Ben. Romantic, secretive and, like most government buildings (including the mad toyshop of the Kremlin), not entirely friendly-looking. Yet behind that fretted scenery it's all much simpler and more logical than it looks. But since few of us are lucky enough to get backstage we have to settle for the looks. They are the product of a disaster, followed by a brilliant rescue operation by two men of genius.

One evening in 1834 Mrs Wright, the Deputy Palace housekeeper, was conducting two visitors over the building, ignoring their complaints of excessive heat – 'I can feel it through my boots' said one. A fire had started in the basement and a few hours later the whole palace was ablaze. By morning it was a smoking ruin. The whole city, it seemed, flocked to the spectacle, half-shocked, half-elated by its grandeur. Among the eye-witnesses was Turner, whose watercolours done on the spot – the pages still blotched with his speed – can be seen in the British Museum, and Charles Barry the young architect who was to win the competition for its rebuilding. His plan was brilliantly simple – a top-lit central lobby placed as a hub and serving the House of Commons to the east and the House of Lords to the west, and made octagonal in shape to disguise a slight change of axis between the river bank and Parliament Square – and all concealed within a complex of courtyards, committee rooms, offices and residences, totalling eight acres in extent. Work started in 1840 and continued for more than twenty years. The style, chosen by Parliament, was Gothic, partly out of respect for the Abbey nearby, partly because it seemed more 'English', partly because it was fast becoming more fashionable. To help him with the detail Barry engaged Augustus Welby Pugin – then only twenty-two years old – a well-born, physically delicate, Roman Catholic church architect who had worked at Windsor Castle and Covent Garden and ran a Gothic carving business. For nearly twenty years he was to work on the building, designing everything from doors and windows, to pinnacles and mullions, lamp brackets and inkstands, floor tiles, carpets and wallpapers – over 2,000 drawings alone for the House of Lords – until, crazed with overwork and exhaustion, he died.

Luckily for us the building's *tour de force* – the main public entrance suite – is not out-of-bounds. It is planned by Barry as a series of visual surprises – first the cramped darkness of the porch, then suddenly a chill breath on the cheek and, at the foot of a flight of steps, Westminster Hall, lofty, dim, echoing, empty 'as if exhausted' (in David Piper's words) 'by occasions'. Designed and built around 1400 by Henry Yevele – the architect of the Abbey nave – it has seen use as a Court of Justice, for the trials of Thomas More and Charles I, and as a seventeenth-century market – Pepys bought a clean shirt there after walking the streets after the Great

Fire of London. Today, filled to the brim with silence, it seems like a great funeral car lying in wait. Straight ahead and up more steps is St Stephen's Hall (once the House of Commons) restored by Barry and lined with faded mural paintings of historical events. (Spare them a look, for nobody else will.) Finally one arrives in the great octagon lobby – high, glittering, splendidly decorated. Here – never mind the subsequent arguments as to who actually did what – both architects can take their bow: Barry for the sequence of spaces, Pugin for the richness of their detail and colour. The partnership had been a tricky one but the result is a masterpiece – one of the best-known and best-loved buildings in the world.

Highgate Cemetery

Highgate, romantically landscaped and packed tight with the famous dead, has been described as London's Père Lachaise. It is one of the seven great commercial cemeteries built round London in the 1830s and '40s. It was owned and laid out in 1836 by the London Cemetery Company and in its day was highly profitable – so profitable that an eastern extension connected by a tunnel was opened in 1854 and a nursery garden business was started.

The client architect was Stephen Geary, an inventive specialist in pubs and gin-palaces and with a taste for theatre. Not for him the pediments and columns of Kensal Green. He plumped for Gothic gloom with Egyptian overtones. Centrepiece of the cemetery is the catacombs – an ingenious two-level design dominated by the pyramidal mausoleum of Julius Beer, designed by J. Oldrid Scott in the style of Halicarnassus. This is the largest but not the oddest of memorials. Nearly 200,000 people are buried here and some of them are remembered by the most eccentric curiosities – a marble piano, a life-size statue, a fireman's helmet, a recumbent mastiff. Notables include Queen Victoria's official horse slaughterer, Charles (Dog-Show) Cruft, Foyle the bookseller, 'Hutch' the cabaret artist; the architects J.B. Papworth, John Brydon and Edward Blore, and Geary himself; writers George Eliot, John Galsworthy, Radclyffe Hall, Arthur Waley; artists Peter de Wint, Fred Goodall, George Richmond, Alfred Stevens; scientists Michael Faraday and Jacob Bronowski; cricketer Fred Lillywhite and boxer Tom Sayers; philosopher Karl Marx; Elizabeth Siddal, model and wife of Rossetti; Richard Smith, inventor of Hovis and Albert Barratt the sweet manufacturer.

As the cemetery filled profits began to fall. By 1970 it was running at a loss, maintenance could no longer be afforded and in 1975 the West cemetery was closed and abandoned to the undergrowth, to the foxes and to vandals. Luckily a group of local enthusiasts has come to the rescue – the Highgate Cemetery Trust – and its members, all volunteers, are gradually restoring this remarkable Valhalla to something like its former splendour.

the Catacombs
Highgate Cemetery -

Stanley Gardens

Around ten years ago, our youngest daughter got married and moved into a flat in Stanley Gardens. A visit to see her there was our first view of this impressively scaled street that lies on the axis of St Peter's Church – almost the last classical-style church to be built in London. The architect for both Stanley Gardens and the Church was Thomas Allom. It was completed in 1857 at a cost of £5,500 and its cupola and pillared porch still command the heights of Notting Hill with confidence and dignity.

The gardens down which it authoritatively gazes are lined with powerfully modelled houses, pedimented, rusticated, bow-windowed and corniced, that hold their own with total ease. Thomas Allom, architect to the developer C.H. Blake, began Stanley Gardens (named after the Earl of Derby, Prime Minister in 1852) following the models of neighbouring layouts, but brought his own talent for scenic composition, his love of architectural display and his affection for the Italianate style – with spectacular results: so grand it looks like a slice of Leningrad. Lavish use of materials, giant projections and recessions, profusely decorated interiors show there was plenty of money about. The residents – usually about nine per house, including, say, three servants – were mostly professional and middle-class, plus a few Girls' Schools. Blake himself lived at No 21 until rich enough to move to No 2 Stanley Crescent, one of the grandest houses in the area. Let nobody grudge him his success. The estate made him rich but it does him credit, too.

Stanley Gardens - W.11.

County Hall

Few of us like Town Halls much. Too pompous, too self-important, too expensive-looking. They always look as if they knew what was good for us. They are not buildings that seem willing to listen. I believe County Hall to be a rare exception. Though facing north-ish it seems always sunny. The curve in the middle is friendly. The steeply tiled roof is homely, the architecture well-cut without being stiff.

It's about sixty years old. The London County Council which inherited in the 1890s the management of London's affairs – education, social services, drainage, transport and the like – was housed at the time in more than a score of separate buildings. In 1905 it decided to buy its present site on the south-east corner of Westminster Bridge – then a collection of warehouses, workshops and mudflats. A two-stage architectural competition was mounted, assessed by Norman Shaw, Aston Webb and W.E. Riley (the LCC's official architect). To the chagrin of many distinguished architect competitors, it was won by a young and unknown architect called Ralph Knott – partly because it was (to quote the assessors) 'entirely without costly and unnecessary features'. (In those days columns, carved voussoirs and cornices, elaborate chimneys and lofty cupolas were not regarded as either.) A new river wall and public walkway were included, the foundation stone laid in March 1912 and, although delayed by the war, it was formally opened in 1922. The plan is symmetrical with the Council Chamber placed in the centre of flanking courtyards and the most important rooms ranged round the recessed crescent of the river front. For three years – during the run-up to the South Bank Exhibition 1951 – I visited this building virtually every day (our partnership with the LCC, particularly on the engineering side, was very close) – and grew to love its interminable vaulted corridors and robust panelling and parquet. As one of the advisers of the Historic Buildings Committee I go there regularly still and enjoy the clarity – once learned – and logic of the internal layout. Somehow Knott and Riley between them control this enormous sprawling building and endow it with its own personality. Good materials strongly used, consistency of detail, avoidance of the slick – all the old excellent rules make this building something of a masterpiece that has matured but never got run-down. We all know the faults endemic to local government – top-heavy bureaucracy, indecision, political in-fighting, dilatoriness – but where else in the world would you find a municipal HQ so free from shabbiness and squalor?

Holly Village

Among the shrubberies at the southern tip of Highgate Cemetery a group of curious little cottages – half-Hansel and Gretel, half-Victorian rectory – can be glimpsed having a sort of witches' picnic around a well-kept lawn. From a distance they are picturesque enough and as you approach them they manage to distil a certain sort of sinister charm. They were built to house, though never received, the workers on the adjoining Holly Lodge Estate. They are symmetrically placed and similar in design but each is different in the detail of the ornament which plays rather grimly over their polychromatic façades. Inside they are a bit dark – the ceilings too high and, again, the detail is idiosyncratic and heavily playful. The architect was Henry Darbishire, a man who specialised, by preference, in designing tenements for the poor of Victorian London. Here he really let fly. The best materials everywhere, fretted timber trellis, carved capitals, sculptured windowheads. The client, so the plaque over the entrance informs you, was Angela Burdett-Coutts, one of the most remarkable women of an age now celebrated for remarkable women.

Angela came of a rich family. She was tall and thin with a melancholy cast to her expression, but she was thoughtful, serious, intelligent and possessed a will of iron. At the age of twenty-three she inherited from her grandfather, Thomas Coutts the banker, his entire estate – the equivalent today of some £30,000,000. There were no other legacies, nothing for her mother or her father – Sir Francis, that Byronic Radical darling of the people who in 1810 had gone to the Tower for his principles – nothing for her brother nor her four sisters. Nothing. She decided to leave home at once in the company of her devoted governess and to spend her life and her money improving the lives of those less fortunate than herself. She achieved this with such success that she was made a Baroness in 1871 and at her death at the age of ninety-two she was hailed everywhere and was almost as celebrated and beloved as Queen Victoria herself. She fought without difficulty the queues of importunate young men who sought her hand, reserving her affections for her governess and later for the Duke of Wellington. They corresponded warmly – sometimes twice a day – and Angela actually proposed marriage but the Duke, then aged seventy-seven, was too old, too deaf and too tired to face it. She turned for consolation to her philanthropy – workers' housing (by Darbishire) in Bethnal Green and Bermondsey, assistance to emigrants, paying for a sewer, a home for the prostitutes who shoaled around her front door nightly in Piccadilly. She sent a drying machine to the Crimea, a cotton gin to the Gold Coast, a paddle-steamer to the Zambesi (to help Livingstone) and a corrugated iron church to British Columbia. Help was provided, not as a hand-out which she regarded as degrading, but where her researches showed it most needed – whether it was teachers or arrowroot, seed potatoes or trained midwives. In all this she relied closely upon the advice of Charles Dickens, another of her 'heroes'.

If this gives a picture of a dull, drably dressed, sanctimonious prig, that would be the reverse of the truth. She enjoyed her money, bought her clothes in Paris, entertained extravagantly and travelled abroad in considerable state. When in 1877 the Turko-Russian war broke out she appointed as her organiser a sparky young man – a protégé of hers for some time – called Ashmead Bartlett. At the age of sixty-six (he was thirty-three), and to the horror of her friends and the raised eyebrows of the Queen, she married him. It worked out well enough. He was an MP, a horse-breeder, a man-about-town. She continued her work. Sadly, little physical remains. The great Columbia Market project is demolished. Holly Lodge and the gardens in which these little houses were built is a housing estate. A few street names remain in Bermondsey to commemorate her name, and this spiky little cluster in Highgate. She slipped away into the shadows as quietly as she had come.

The Royal Opera House, Covent Garden

Nobody calls it that of course. You go either to the 'opera' or to 'Covent Garden' – never to the Royal Opera House. I never went at all till 1952 – my family were not opera-lovers – when I was commissioned to do the sets for Sir William Walton's *Troilus and Cressida* (libretto Christopher Hassall, conductor Sir Malcolm Sargent, producer George Devine). It was my second opera – *Alceste* at Glyndebourne being my first – and I was totally unnerved by the grandeur of the event, but, as so often happens, I was carried to safety by the professionalism of my colleagues. The singers, Richard Lewis and Magda Laszlo, were old friends from *Alceste*. George Devine also I knew well. William Walton, dry, amused, apparently casual but deeply professional, was throughout a loyal supporter and Clementine Glock (who painted the scenery) kept me clear of inexperienced decisions. Four sets were required – outside a temple, the besieged camp, the city penthouse of Pandarus, another part of the camp. Sadly, and to me inexplicably, for the music was magical, the opera received no more than a polite reception and it is seldom revived. The experience of working in that splendid theatre was, however, an excitement still to be remembered. Every time I go there and enter that auditorium I get a lift of the spirits – a silent tribute to the work of the architect E.M. Barry.

Barry's theatre is the fifth to occupy this site. Both its immediate predecessors were burned down, the loss of Albano's spectacular interior after only nine years of existence being particularly tragic. Crowned with a great saucer dome, it was one of the largest theatres in Europe and was built by relays of workmen labouring day and night over four months. But on 5 March 1856 it was burned to the ground. Pessimists who believed that was that, were proved wrong. Mr Gye, the manager, returned overnight from Paris, conducted Queen Victoria round the ruins and gave orders for an immediate replacement. Within a year work had started and within seven months it was open, thanks to the builders, Lucas Brothers. Barry – the son of Sir Charles – based his design closely on Albano's but turned the axis at right angles and the auditorium is slightly smaller, the stage raked and the colour scheme simpler. Minor improvements continued over the years and a couple of years ago a block of respectfully faced new rehearsal rooms, workshop and back stage facilities have been added at the back, but basically it remains a triumphant, Victorian achievement, the credit for which must go to Gye, Albano, Barry and the Lucas Brothers. The old operatic rivals – Her Majesty's in Haymarket and Theatre Royal Drury Lane – dropped out before the First World War and after a struggling inter-war existence under the control of Sir Thomas Beecham, and wartime service as a dance hall, the Royal Opera House seems safely established musically and architecturally among the great opera houses of the world.

The National Theatre

I grew up with this project. My uncle – the actor Lewis Casson – was, with Bernard Shaw, one of the original promoters and I remember the foundation stone being laid just by our present office in Thurloe Place. I saw it laid for the second time in 1951 on the South Bank near the Festival Hall and, later, for the third time, a few hundred yards downstream where it now, at last, stands.

The architects were chosen, as I well remember, by interview with a formidable and sharp-edged committee including Lord Olivier, the first Director. It was – as such things always are – an instructive experience, but in selecting Sir Denys Lasdun as architect the committee was correctly convinced that if a building is to be a work of art it must be under the control of an artist. From the outside it is a strong and deceptively simple building that commands its riverside site. The architects have treated the building like landscape – a stratified rocky outcrop that responds to the geometry of the streets and the river wall and connects at many levels to its surroundings. It has been criticised for its lack of external gaiety – it is built inside and out of grey untreated concrete, deliberately chosen by the architect to evoke the permanent and avoid the slick – and as it faces north there is not much play of light and shade to enliven the strong modelling of terraces and stairtowers. It is sad, too, that it had to be kept back from the river wall. (Architecture always behaves well with its toes in the water – look at Udaipur, Leningrad or Venice.) But inside it works a treat and Londoners have quickly learned to use it and love it. The foyers are always crammed – young people squatting on the floor, tiny bands banging away under the staircases, plenty of bars and vantage points. Sometimes it's quite difficult to tear oneself from the party to see the play.

Today of course, the architecture attracts less comment than the content. The building has been awarded the nicest of all compliments, affectionate public acceptance. The National Theatre, like Covent Garden, is one of the Arts Council's flagships. It eats, in some people's view, a disproportionately large portion of the government's annual subsidy to the arts. Every art-supporting government faces this conflict between 'centres of established excellence' – or 'art as glory' – and off-centre experimentalism, i.e. 'art as welfare'. (Dictatorships seem to prefer the latter, democracies the former.) Centres of excellence, say the critics, stifle change. Art as welfare, say the other critics, is usually self-indulgent and sacrifices quality. The debate continues.

Harrow

'I love Harrow', said Sir John Betjeman recently, 'first because it is not Eton and secondly because I believe I was at school there . . . in spirit if not in fact.'

I find no surprise that he should say so . . . and also for two reasons: first because it is one of the most complete, compact and unspoiled complexes of Victorian architecture in the country, and second because it is visibly, if not in fact, the capital city of Metroland – that strange Arcady that was the product, some fifty years ago, of a partnership between the Metropolitan Railway and the speculative builder. To Londoners its silhouette is as familiar as Hampstead or Sydenham yet it looks somehow as mysterious and lonely as Glastonbury. The village church has been there since the Middle Ages, but it is the school, founded for local boys in 1571, which, like a feudal landlord, has protected the hill's privacy from the the slow tide of gabled roofs and factory estates by which it is surrounded, and has created the identity of Harrow. That school of 'Forty Years On' and the shallow boater was created later between 1850 and 1885 by two fearsome headmasters, Dr Vaughan and Dr Butler, and it is to these two that we owe the extraordinary collection of school buildings, striped, blood-red, hard-edged, pinnacled and menacing which must have terrified every new boy out of his wits. Virtually all the great Victorian architects had a go here – not always on their best form: Gilbert Scott (the Chapel and the Vaughan Library), William Burges (the Speech Room), Basil Champneys (the Butler Museum), A.W. Blomfield and Aston Webb (Chapel alterations), E.S. Prior (the new music room and various boarding houses) and, most prolific of all, Charles Forster Hayward (the Science Schools, the Sanatorium and a group of boarding houses). Hayward, like one other busy Harrow architect, W.C. Marshall, had a housemaster brother which no doubt had its local advantages.

Yet there's more to Harrow than the School. St Mary's Church, despite Gilbert Scott's merciless restoration, is worth a leisurely visit and the High Street and The Green are as quiet and friendly as a small west country town. In Peterborough Road and on the south side of the hill, some splendid suburban mansions survive and for lovers of the fantastic there's a mad chalet in Harrow Park designed by J.T. Walford (1883) which would have delighted King Ludwig himself. And there's always that view – wide-ranging from the churchyard or glimpsed, like the sea in a fishing port, between the shoulders of houses and garden walls, that seems to distil a pale, pearly light, limitless yet contained, as if Harrow and you were captured within a dome of glass.

A sketch book does not warrant a Bibliography but I would like to acknowledge the help
I have received in particular from the following books and authors:

The Companion Guide to London, David Piper (Collins 1964)
The Companion Guide to Outer London, Simon Jenkins (Collins 1981)
Victorian London, Priscilla Metcalfe (Cassell 1972)
Also:
London and the Exhibition, Cyrus Redding (Henry G. Bohn 1851)
Turner, Jack Lindsay (Panther 1973)
The Buildings of England (London, Volume I), Nikolaus Pevsner (Penguin 1957)
The Victorian Society Annual (1968–9)
The Royal College of Music: a Centenary Record (1982)
The Thurloe Estate, Dorothy Stroud (Country Life 1965)
National Portrait Gallery Souvenir Guide (1977)
Victorian Buildings of London 1837–1887, Gavin Stamp & Colin Amery (Architectural Press
    1980)
Arts & Crafts Architecture, Peter Davey (Architectural Press 1980)
Marble Halls (Victoria & Albert Museum Exhibition Catalogue), John Physick & Michael
    Darby (1973)
A Revolution in London Housing, Susan Beattie (G.L.C. & Architectural Press 1980)
The Growth of Victorian London, Donald J. Olsen (Batsford 1976)
London 1900 – Architectural Design Profiles 13 (Vol. 18, No. 5–6, 1978)
Sir John Soane, John Summerson (Art & Technics 1952)
Edwardian Architecture, Alastair Service (Thames & Hudson 1977)
Semi-Detached London, Alan A. Jackson (George Allen & Unwin 1973)
Pugin, John Glen Harries (Shire Publications 1973)
The Houses of Parliament, James Pope-Hennessy (Michael Joseph 1975)
The London Building World of the Eighteen-Sixties (Walter Neurath Memorial Lecture 1973)
    John Summerson (Thames & Hudson 1973)
John Nash, John Summerson (George Allen & Unwin 1935)
Notting Hill in bygone days, Florence Gladstone & Ashley Barker (Anne Bingley 1969)
London Night & Day, ed. Sam Lambert Illustrated Osbert Lancaster (Architectural Press 1951)
Paintings, Prints & Drawings of Harrow on the Hill, 1562–1899, Alan W. Ball (London Borough
    of Harrow 1978)
Historic Buildings in London (An inventory of historic buildings owned by the G.L.C.)
    (Academy Editions 1975)
Lady Unknown, Edna Healey (Sidgwick & Jackson 1978)
Kensington & Chelsea, William Gaunt (Batsford 1975)
Architecture in Britain 1530–1830 (The Pelican History of Art), John Summerson (Penguin 1953)
The Architectural Association 1847–1947 John Summerson (Pleiades Books 1947)
The Victorian Society Annual (1981)
G.L.C. Survey of London (Northern Kensington Vol. XXXVII) (Athlone Press 1972)
The Queen's London (Cassell & Co. 1897)
Alfred Waterhouse and The National History Museum, Mark Girouard (British Museum (Natural
    History) 1981)